The New York Times

BEST OF THE WEEK SERIES 2
FRIDAY CROSSWORDS

First published in the United States by St. Martin's Griffin,
an imprint of St. Martin's Publishing Group

THE NEW YORK TIMES BEST OF THE WEEK SERIES 2: FRIDAY CROSSWORDS.
Copyright © 2021 by The New York Times Company. All rights reserved.
Printed in China. For information, address St. Martin's Publishing Group,
120 Broadway, New York, NY 10271.

www.stmartins.com

All of the puzzles that appear in this work were originally published in
The New York Times from May 3, 2013, to November 15, 2013; from
April 4, 2014, to April 13, 2014; or from September 4, 2020, to December 25, 2020.
Copyright © 2013, 2014, 2020 by The New York Times Company.
All rights reserved. Reprinted by permission.

ISBN 978-1-250-80332-0

Our books may be purchased in bulk for promotional, educational, or business use.
Please contact your local bookseller or the Macmillan Corporate and Premium Sales Department
at 1-800-221-7945, extension 5442, or by email at MacmillanSpecialMarkets@macmillan.com.

First Edition: 2021

10 9 8 7 6 5 4 3 2 1

The New York Times

BEST OF THE WEEK SERIES 2: FRIDAY CROSSWORDS
50 Challenging Puzzles

Edited by Will Shortz

ST. MARTIN'S GRIFFIN
NEW YORK

Looking for more Hard Crosswords?

The New York Times

The #1 Name in Crosswords

ACROSS

1 Meme you've seen a thousand times, maybe
7 Theater section
10 Adele or Ed Sheeran
14 Nobel Prize winner whose name should ring a bell?
16 What a lock on a bridge can symbolize
17 Trucker's tracker
18 In deep water
19 ___ class (provider of an aerobic workout)
20 128 oz.
21 Many June celebrants
22 Land east of the Eastern Desert
25 Drink that may contain aspartame
27 Sleep inits.
28 First winner of the Nebula Award for Best Novel, 1965
29 Year, in Portuguese
30 Vanilla-flavored drink
33 Golden ___ (vanilla-flavored snack)
34 Congresswoman who said "I want to be remembered as the only woman who ever voted to give women the right to vote"
36 "I got this!"
37 "Hold your horses!"
38 They might come in saucers, for short
39 Notice
40 Athlete in the N.B.A.'s Southwest Div.
41 Largest order of animals on earth, with over 350,000 species
43 Tears
46 Puget Sound predators
47 ___ + Shay, Grammy-winning country duo

49 "Shoot!"
51 Easternmost point of the Silk Road
52 Vacation destination
55 Juul, e.g., informally
56 High-level criminal?
57 Seat of Washoe County
58 Hubbub
59 Nutritious breakfast cereal

DOWN

1 Lips
2 "Oh What a Circus" musical
3 Less bright
4 Like the families portrayed on "Gilmore Girls" and "Full House"
5 Vacation destination
6 It is avoided while playing it
7 ___ prima (painting technique)
8 Hipsters
9 Rating for "Full House"
10 Movie mall cop
11 She took a seat to take a stand
12 "Ta-da!"
13 One of about 500 million needed to fill an Olympic swimming pool
15 Brightest star in Lyra
21 "Shucks!"
23 Noodle
24 Very big
26 Going away
28 A bit crazy
30 Hockey face-off site
31 Hoot and holler
32 Doesn't move another inch
33 In a mean way?
34 Underwear brand
35 Way off
39 Letters typed with the right ring finger
42 Dance seen in 2-Down
43 Expensive beer chaser?
44 Counts' counterparts
45 Lift
48 About
50 Wedding dress that's often red
52 DVR manufacturer
53 Main ingredient in a hurricane cocktail
54 ___ TV (WarnerMedia channel)

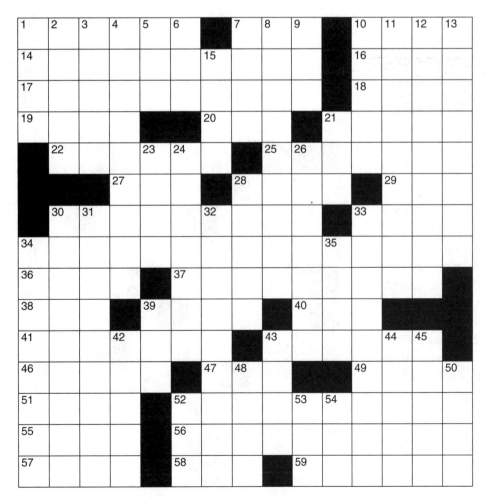

by Brian Thomas

ACROSS

1 Fans of the Bible?
11 It's hardly a breath of fresh air
15 Apartment units
16 Where to visit the U.S.S. Arizona Memorial
17 Necked, jocularly
18 Sort (through)
19 Perspectives
20 Starters
22 Bobs and weaves
23 Phone-unlocking option
25 Pictures
27 "Auntie," on the telly
30 Dreaded examination
32 Like bells
33 Achilles' heel, e.g.
35 Lap-sitter
36 Solution for a chef, maybe
37 Not on time, but that's OK
41 Talent, in slang
42 Sister language of Thai
43 Member of the House of Saud, e.g.
44 ___ nut
45 Cicely ___, 2020 Television Academy Hall of Fame inductee
47 Seventh of 24
48 Plot device that prompts a protagonist to piece things together
50 Right columns?
52 Roar from a crowd
53 Proverbial back-breaker
55 King ___
59 "My, my!"
61 Get out of here!
63 Miguel in "Coco," por ejemplo
64 Sweet Indian beverage
65 "Rock or Bust" rockers
66 One who's about ready to go out?

DOWN

1 Attention getter
2 Lead-in to culture
3 Unfortunate thing to be out of
4 Nets
5 Alternative to 7Up
6 Like the circle in the 7Up logo
7 Intermittently
8 Dandy
9 Trickery
10 Tick off
11 Title of hits by Abba and Rihanna
12 Something that might be sacrificed at the altar?
13 "Never mind!"
14 Full of grit
21 Unite
24 Jaguars, e.g.
26 Trickery
27 With whom you might have a Snapchat streak, informally
28 Bad spells
29 Liquid paper?
31 Where eyeglasses and espresso machines were invented
34 & 36 What plasma may be removed from
38 "Check"
39 It comes before overtime
40 Slice of life, maybe
45 Kind of bone near the tibia and fibula
46 "___ done!"
48 Game site
49 Objects
51 Literally, "law"
54 Face covering of a sort
56 Big producer of speakers
57 Santa ___, Calif.
58 Surrounded by
60 Nonfiction film, informally
62 Really jump out

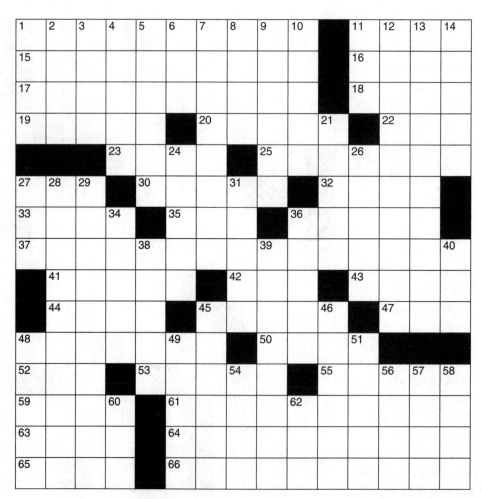

by Caitlin Reid and Erik Agard

ACROSS

1 Part of a boot
7 Purina product
14 "Finished!"
15 "You wish!"
16 Young raptor
17 Highs and lows, e.g.
18 Much-discussed immigration measure first introduced in 2001
20 Silver
21 Ape whose name comes from Malay for "man"
23 "I reckon"
24 Company that makes vegan alternatives to beef and sausage
29 The Liberty Tree and others
32 Observe Yom Kippur, e.g.
33 Adidas alternative
34 Vacation locale for President Gerald Ford
35 Actress Elisabeth
36 Hauled
37 Tennis's Kournikova
38 Wails
39 Pat on the back, maybe
40 Upright
41 "You have a point . . ."
42 No-win situations
44 Put on a black coat?
46 Nice things to get on the back, but not on the face
47 Cleaned up, in a way
50 Frenzied
55 Area including Arkansas, Louisiana, Mississippi and Texas
57 Capital of the onetime Republic of the Rio Grande
58 "It sounds to me like . . ."
59 Follows, as advice
60 Rubberized, maybe
61 "Bug"

DOWN

1 One-to-one, say
2 Congresswoman Ilhan
3 Lucky thing to hit in Ping-Pong
4 Fountain option
5 Windflower
6 Fortification-breaching bomb
7 Crew leader, informally
8 Former U.N. secretary general Kofi ___ Annan
9 Linger
10 Subject of a classic black, white and red poster
11 Earth, to us
12 Many a tournament
13 Occident
15 Subject in the purview of the Federal Communications Commission
19 In-tents experiences?
22 Method of attack
24 Opera's Don Pedro and Don Pasquale, e.g.
25 Shared values
26 "Just watch me do it!"
27 Race cars, typically
28 Soupçon
30 Chop
31 Blind spots?
36 "Full Frontal With Samantha Bee" network
40 Typographer's gap
43 Where water samples may be tested, informally
45 Luke Skywalker or Han Solo
47 Sportscaster Andrews
48 First queen of Carthage
49 Member of the South Asian diaspora
51 Hangings in la Galleria degli Uffizi
52 Place to find the birds and the bees?
53 One with tens of millions of Instagram followers, maybe
54 Part of an obstacle course
56 Race unit

by Anne and Daniel Larsen

4

ACROSS

1 The "stuf" in Double Stuf Oreos
6 Keeps track of a count, maybe
10 Seoul music
14 Balloon material
15 Deal breaker?
16 Wander
17 High anxiety?
19 "You don't need to tell me what happened"
20 Junior
21 Lowest rating in showbiz's Ulmer Scale
23 Kind of paste in East Asian cuisine
26 Local boundaries?
29 Prefix with saccharide or glyceride
31 Basketball highlight, informally
32 Sets to zero, in a way
34 "Star Wars" spinoff set five years after Emperor Palpatine's fall
37 It's difficult to go against
38 Force feed
39 Ones diving right into their work?
41 Perfume
42 Rump
43 Shape of some hooks
44 "__ but a scratch!"
45 Mythological hunter turned into a stag
48 Infantile affliction
50 Dreams
55 Subject of J. J. Thomson's "plum pudding" model
57 Concept in artificial intelligence
60 Scrutinize, with "over"
61 "Chariots of Fire" filming locale
62 Half-bird, half-woman creature

63 __ Choice Awards
64 Spots in which to lie low
65 Collide into the side of

DOWN

1 Keep the beat, in a way
2 Tear
3 Verb with a circumflex
4 [More tuna, please!]
5 Avant-garde
6 Card game shout
7 Berlioz's "Queen __" Scherzo
8 N.Y.C. event on the last Sunday in June
9 Teatro alla __
10 Kardashian family member
11 Rumps
12 Monthly releases of a sort
13 Hymnbook holder
18 Giggle bit
22 How a mysterious figure may disappear
24 "Be serious!"
25 Shape, informally
27 Is biased
28 Some sensitive info, for short
29 60
30 What Ralph Nader did in 2000, 2004 and 2008
33 Passionate, confident sort, they say
34 Actor Stanley
35 "It's __ from me"
36 Something you can't have while standing up

37 "It'll __ you"
40 Bio class subject
46 Quoted
47 Sister channel of HGTV
49 "Good" or "ill" thing
51 Shot in the dark
52 Sub
53 "Fantasy Focus" podcast airer
54 Lump near a lash
55 On point
56 The smallest one is called a minimus
58 Who joins Gryffindor's Quidditch team in "Harry Potter and the Order of the Phoenix"
59 Good people to know

by Rachel Fabi

ACROSS

1 Shade similar to honey
6 Hinge (on)
10 Early stage for some bugs?
14 City near Memphis
15 Self-evident
17 See 25-Across
18 Whom one might address as "sensei"
19 Host of the first World Table Tennis Championships: Abbr.
20 Dress
22 Reason for a donation
23 Two-wheelers
25 With 17-Across, "Giant" actor of 1956
26 Stewing, say
27 Deliberately sink
31 One hand washing the other, so to speak
34 Red peg, in the game Battleship
35 It's hard to fight
36 "Seems likely"
37 Recipient of a "Brava!"
38 Ending with Black or brack
39 Admissions considerations
41 Whistlers of a sort
44 Possible uses for Bundt pans
45 "Isle of Dogs" director Anderson
46 Rules of conduct
49 Sphere of influence
52 Core exercise
53 Neighbor of Scorpius in the sky
54 Modify so as to bypass a device's restrictions, in hacker lingo
56 Things opened at spas
58 Talus
59 I I I
60 "Seeded" or "unseeded" grocery choices
61 Growl like an angry dog
62 Aromatic herb

DOWN

1 Tips
2 Dessert preceder
3 Event with a room full of people making a row
4 "Take heed, __ summer comes or cuckoo-birds do sing": "The Merry Wives of Windsor"
5 Urban kind of bar or garden
6 Epitome of sharpness
7 "Brass"
8 Serving of kielbasa or knackwurst
9 Hebrew for "day"
10 Volcanic rock
11 Some famous last words
12 Deuces, e.g.
13 One of Yellowstone's 2.2+ million
16 Eastern gambling mecca
21 Overdrafts?
24 Of yore, of yore
25 Adam Smith and David Hume, e.g.
27 Bird feeder fill
28 Socialists, e.g.
29 Air on Twitch, say
30 Info on a flight tracker app
31 Classic cocoa powder brand
32 Horatian compilation
33 Most Super Bowl M.V.P.'s
37 Ration
40 Place for an ace
42 Denim and chino
43 Opposite of bother
46 Something to try first
47 Fall person, perhaps
48 Senator Ben from Nebraska
49 Cracked
50 "__ thanks!"
51 Triathlete's need
52 Drudge
55 Late justice known for powerful dissents, for short
57 Sound at a fireworks display

by Debbie Ellerin

ACROSS

1 Student who might take a crash course?
10 Chills
15 Direct kind of fight
16 Apply
17 Leftovers from a Greek salad
18 Burton who hosted "Reading Rainbow"
19 Dating app blurb
20 True
22 "Yesterday, I __ a clock. It was very time-consuming" (groaner joke)
23 Bad marks for a high schooler
25 1/768 of a gal.
26 "Haven't the foggiest"
28 Silently acknowledges
30 __ Flakes (old Post cereal)
32 Hide
33 Winter airplane need
34 Darts
36 Homes all over the planet?
40 Look for people to scam online
41 __ di Mare (Italian fashion label)
43 Up (or down) for something
46 Obituary word
47 More warm, in a way
48 Slangy response to a knock at the door
50 Round-bottomed vessel
52 Batik artist, e.g.
53 Shirt protector
54 Beckett title character
56 Bruiser
57 Hwy. through St. Paul, Minn.
59 Gymnastics rings feat with arms fully extended

63 Locale of the Île de la Cité
64 "Take some time to think"
65 Minds
66 They provide a clearer picture

DOWN

1 Taking Back Sunday or Dashboard Confessional
2 Printed cotton fabrics
3 Party bowlful with a sour cream base
4 Mo. for Guy Fawkes Day
5 Astronaut Jemison
6 Boomer at a concert
7 Puts away
8 Elated

9 Promising
10 Pick-up line?
11 __ throwing (faddish sport)
12 Where Colin Kaepernick played college football
13 Hazards for high heels
14 Zoom
21 Kind of missile
24 Got out
25 Verbally attacked
27 >:-(
29 Stock market sector, for short
31 Mimicking
35 Part of many a tree swing
37 Chicago-to-Indianapolis dir.
38 Zero

39 Infuses with
42 Parts of a record
43 Prez with the same initials as an N.Y.C. landmark
44 "It all makes sense now"
45 Connection to the underworld
49 __ Scott College, one of the Seven Sisters of the South
51 Tribe that traditionally spoke Chiwere
55 Trade gossip
58 Period, with "the"
60 Japanese electronics giant
61 Y.M.C.A. course
62 Norma McCorvey's alias in a famous court case

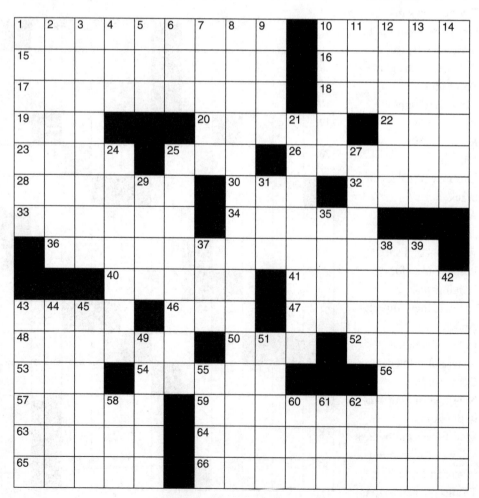

by Sam Buchbinder

ACROSS

1 Graduation props?
7 Where gowns are worn, for short
10 Eponymous Dutch town
14 One of a tribe of mythical warriors
15 Showboaty home run celebrations
17 The People's Princess, to the people
18 Statement of readiness
19 "Win some, lose some"
21 Singer Bareilles
22 Key chain?
23 It's not merely a yen
26 Actor in "The Office" and "The Hangover"
31 Mentally exhilarating experience
35 Seconds, say
36 "It's nobody's fault"
40 Inits. at the top of some brackets
41 Conclusive proof provider
42 Enormous in proportion
46 Place to buy and sell online
47 Jazz fan, presumably
49 Cheek or lip
53 "Called it!"
58 Bygone mode of transportation
59 Defector, perhaps
60 What keywords are used for
61 Starter follower
62 Big __ (40-Across conference)
63 Number often seen before a plus sign
64 Repudiate

DOWN

1 Shuts down
2 City in which Malcolm X was born
3 Former presidential candidate who wrote "Only the Super-Rich Can Save Us!"
4 The "king of kings," per a famous sonnet
5 Nuclear fuel containers
6 Huff
7 Most valuable player awards?
8 Go on tangent after tangent
9 Didn't merely peek
10 "We All Love __: Celebrating the First Lady of Song" (2007 tribute)
11 Plate, e.g.
12 Brutes
13 Winter hrs. in Yellowstone
16 Peach part
20 Used as a lair
24 A few minutes after your Lyft arrives, say
25 What can come before long
27 Incompetent execs
28 Easy pace
29 G.I. rations, for short
30 Text message status
31 Prince in "Frozen"
32 Latin "Lo!"
33 Smoothie bar stock
34 Group electing officers in Sept., maybe
37 Whiff
38 Sellout
39 "Remove __" (in-app come-on)
43 Zoom call status
44 Lago di Como locale
45 Door or window frame
48 Depend (on)
50 Belligerent, in British slang
51 Cousin of a mole
52 Dutch painter Jan
53 Actress Malone of the "Hunger Games" films
54 Supermarket IDs
55 Word before check . . . or a pattern alternative to a check
56 Opposite of disregard
57 Hilton competitor
58 Half of a jazz duo

by Damon Gulczynski

ACROSS

1 Cable news lineup
6 Only character with the same name in both "Rent" and "La Bohème"
10 Some urgent messages, in brief
14 Dramatic device
15 What's before after, at the end?
16 Kaplan course subj.
17 "That's enough for now"
19 Singular
20 Most promising slate of candidates
21 Decision spot
22 Dark half
23 Sexy
24 One who might have a brush with fame?
26 Jobs at Apple, once
27 Prom night worry
29 Puzzle solver's cry
30 Legal pad alternative
33 Lightly lined apparel
34 Batting equipment?
35 Cost-of-living fig.
36 Array on a screen
37 The season opener?
38 Author who was a childhood friend of Harper Lee
40 Filch
41 Melissa Jefferson __ Lizzo
44 Spots for bulbs
45 Celebrity's influence
48 Overhaul
49 Goes in 100%
50 Single piece of underwear, paradoxically
51 Highland slope
52 Background distraction
53 Some are traditional, in brief
54 Steel (oneself)
55 Mount

DOWN

1 Mark
2 Japanese beer brand
3 Camera mentioned in Paul Simon's "Kodachrome" (not a Kodak!)
4 River of Germany
5 Upgrade at a dealership
6 Warrant
7 Singer/actor who narrated 1964's "Rudolph the Red-Nosed Reindeer"
8 Gist
9 Put out
10 Divvy up
11 Autoimmune condition with itchy skin
12 Use of a cushion or a backboard
13 Anne or Jeanne: Abbr.
18 B+ or A-
21 E-tail perk
24 Tree toppers
25 Pine product
26 Pine product
27 Pieces of pomegranate
28 Nightclub of song, familiarly
30 Resource with content in 300+ languages
31 __ school
32 Seeks judgment, in a way
33 Fairy tale patriarch
34 Grp. that watches TV
39 Some may linger
40 Encrusted
41 Be in store
42 Ashton Kutcher's role on "That '70s Show"
43 Longtime senator Specter
45 Who asks "What can I help you with?"
46 Former Bulgarian monarch
47 Omaha relative
48 Tech sch. in upstate N.Y.
49 Initials of the person who said "Fight for the things that you care about, but do it in a way that will lead others to join you"

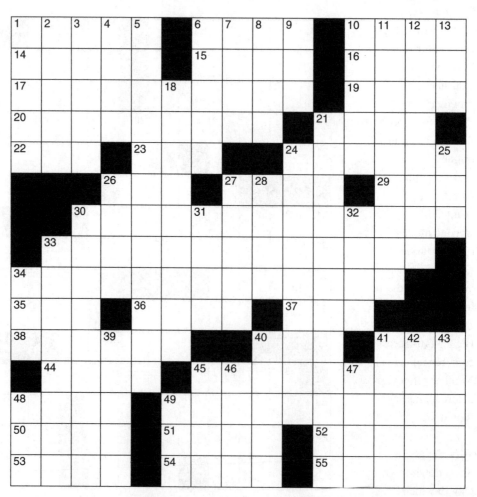

by Robyn Weintraub

by Trenton Charlson

ACROSS

1 Jesus, Mary or Joseph
9 Some Eastern dignitaries
15 Occasion for grilling
16 Something worn for protection
17 Own
18 "Philosophy in the Bedroom" writer, 1795
19 "There's the __"
20 Way to get around in Chicago
22 Schedule abbr.
23 On deck, say
25 Scientist who was friends with Mark Twain
26 Consider
27 Half of Italy
29 Floats are often made with them
31 __ Games, second-largest multisport event after the Olympics
32 Contemptuous, in a way
33 Welcome offering
35 Portraitist's request
36 [Ho-o-o boy, here we go again . . .]
41 Heat-resistant glass
45 Midwest city in the title of a 1942 Glenn Miller #1 hit
46 Margaret __, artist known for painting subjects with big eyes
47 Those in favor
48 Spoils
50 Word with search or witness
51 Open-house org.
52 Acts like a quidnunc
54 Kind of rock
55 Support above a doorway
57 10-year-old boy of comics with glasses and blond hair
59 Unprincipled
60 Words said with a wave
61 Writer who served as a senator in Chile
62 Like wild accusations

DOWN

1 Rhyming descriptor for Obama
2 Turns on
3 River through Victoria Falls
4 Krieger of the U.S. women's soccer team
5 French name meaning "born again"
6 Apotheosize
7 Shoots the breeze
8 Liberal arts college in Boston
9 Sends off
10 Last word of the New Testament
11 Dip for a French dip
12 Youth support group
13 Comedian Mitch who said "I haven't slept for 10 days, because that would be too long"
14 Decreases, in a way?
21 After-shave additive
24 Plants whose name derives from the Greek for "dry"
26 Members of a pantheon
28 Two bells, nautically
30 Allegro
34 Actress Rossellini of "Blue Velvet"
36 When it's light
37 __ Smeal, three-term president of NOW
38 Polo alternative
39 "Bravo!"
40 Flow down a mountain
42 Fine example?
43 Charms
44 Copies, in a way
45 Competitor of Peterson's and Princeton Review
49 Y Y Y Y, on a form
52 Renaissance Faire quaff
53 Cross
56 1989 one-man show
58 Devils' advocate?: Abbr.

ACROSS

1 YouTube star Chamberlain, whom The Atlantic called "the most talked-about teen influencer in the world"
5 Abbr. on a family tree
9 "Dirty Harry" org.
13 Loaded questions?
15 Reacted in wonderment
17 When it's all *finally* over
18 Grade A
19 Hunches
21 Bunches
22 Crafts created on a rotating platform
26 Strip at the beach?
28 Kind of code
29 Quarters abroad, maybe
31 Risen, in a way
33 Sides of a conversion
36 German opposite of "junge"
37 "Thus . . ."
39 Hello or goodbye
40 Lipton competitor
42 Easy-listening music
44 Take a good, long look at yourself?
46 Political __
47 Absolutely crazy
49 Rutherford and Shackleton, for two
51 Figure skating maneuver
52 Buckingham Palace attendant
54 Disney character who sings "Part of Your World"
56 Really bothered
61 Le __ (French port)
62 Satisfies, as with a small snack
63 In case
64 Gender-neutral possessive
65 Pickup order?

DOWN

1 Wane
2 Month after avril
3 Muscleman who co-starred in "Rocky III"
4 Legal fig.
5 More urgent
6 "Still . . ."
7 Makes a big mistake
8 R.O.T.C. group
9 Soup-soaked bread, say
10 Part of an apathetic remark
11 Uncultured sorts
12 Something summoned via a pentagram
14 __ value
16 Spoil, with "on"
20 Had done, as a portrait
22 [Kerplop!]
23 Director of "Get Out" and "Us"
24 Daydreaming, maybe
25 More familiar term for omphaloskeptics
27 PBS-funding org.
30 Stranger
32 Deny
34 "I __ noticed"
35 Sources of tofu
38 Diagnostic computer setting
41 Length of time spent on hold, it often seems
43 Festival de __
45 No longer bothered by
47 Bo-o-oring
48 Kind of medical exam
50 Parties with black lights, maybe
53 ". . . now __ the future"
55 Rent out
57 !, in some programming languages
58 A.C.C. basketball powerhouse
59 Stereotypical cowboy nickname
60 Tamil title

by Aimee Lucido

ACROSS

1 Words that might accompany an outstretched hand
10 Wikipedia articles that need expanding
15 "Look at me go!"
16 "Dear Mama" rapper
17 "You're good"
18 Excited
19 Letter after 53-Across
20 "___ From Queens," comedy series co-created by Awkwafina
21 Physicist Tesla
22 Japanese electronics company bought by Sony in 2002
24 Soup dumpling
26 "That smarts!"
27 Pan . . . or a word that follows pan
29 Soft, squishy material
30 "Charms strike the sight, but merit wins the ___": Pope
31 Word often said after a wild tangent
33 Songs by a recording artist that aren't well known
35 Key of Dvorak's "Serenade for Strings": Abbr.
37 "Think so?"
38 Full throttle
42 Toasts, say
46 Place for a monitor
47 Cousin of "OMG!"
49 Disappointing turnout
50 Park in N.Y.C.: Abbr.
51 Afresh
53 Letter before 19-Across
54 Soy product originally from Indonesia
56 ___ ceiling
58 Mend, in a way
59 I-, for one
60 Line upon arrival
62 Early tablet user
63 Like a cakewalk
64 Response to "Who's there?" that may be unhelpful
65 Stop tinkering with an email

DOWN

1 Ancient undeciphered writing system
2 Heart
3 Take to a pound
4 ___ Balls
5 Mend, in a way
6 Straight shooter?
7 Wrinkle-resistant
8 Hit the jackpot, with "up"
9 They're high up in Chi-Town
10 Risk of drinking coffee or wine
11 Prominent feature of a babirusa ("deer-pig")
12 "I'm good with whatever"
13 Financial rescue
14 Chicken scratchings, say
21 Credit card come-on
23 Too
25 Successful shot from downtown, in basketball lingo
28 Subdue
30 Honker
32 Name so sacred that some refuse to speak it
34 Total inconvenience
36 Most common papal name
38 End of a riddle
39 Lack
40 College football rival of 'Bama
41 Trait of a talented musician
43 Wigs out
44 Provide, as a password
45 Hijiki or arame, in a Japanese restaurant
48 Opposed
51 Like some forests and fog
52 Conforms
55 It may be measured in feet
57 "___ brillig . . ."
60 Not square, once
61 Shape that is both concave and convex

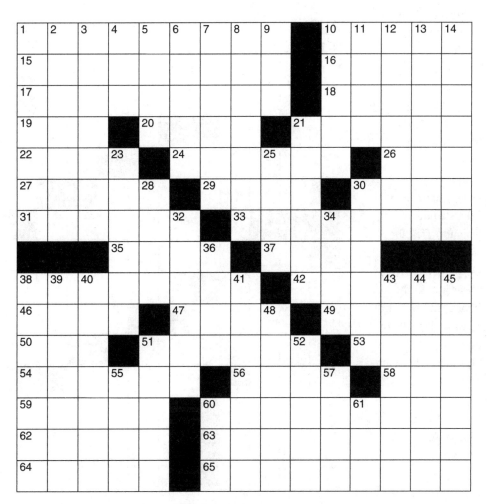

by Sawyer Tabony and Ashton Anderson

ACROSS

1 Catchphrase on "The Simpsons"
10 Not so hot
14 Love poet of old
15 Stage honor
16 Experts in determining the exact shape and size of the earth
17 Court seat
18 Crisp, picturewise
19 Place name in Manhattan
21 CARE, e.g., for short
22 Got
25 Satisfied the munchies
27 Digital identifiers
30 Startled response to "Eek, a mouse!"
31 Avalanche
34 Parched
35 Common activity in couples therapy
38 Off the ___
39 Like presidents with Bibles, maybe
40 Discontinued grocery chain that was once the U.S.'s largest retailer
42 Snuggles
45 Hearty har-hars
48 Like stadiums
50 Counter offer, for short?
51 Goes "Grrrr"
54 "Kiss Me ___ the Phone" (2009 #3 hit)
55 Spanish opposite of odio
57 "Little Rhody," with "the"
60 ___ lives
61 Classic Buster Keaton film set in Civil War times
62 Cut
63 Some terms set by consenting partners

DOWN

1 Childish denial
2 Attention getter
3 Someone to snuggle with
4 Fiver
5 Some campus V.I.P.'s
6 ___ Barnes, W.N.I.T.-winning basketball coach
7 Spanish ___
8 Ashtray fill
9 Burning issue
10 Swarm
11 Many workers on Wall Street, informally
12 Slips and such
13 Cracked, in a way
14 Weekend warrior's cry
20 Uncut
23 Requests made to latecomers, in brief
24 Game in which the object is to end with zero points
26 Psst! Don't pass it on!
28 Burgeoned
29 Old English dialect
32 "An Officer and a Gentleman" star, 1982
33 German philosopher Bloch
35 Hiker's bagful
36 Annoying thing to hear in a movie theater
37 Queens's ___ Field
38 Dolce's partner in fashion
41 One parent of a mixed-breed "poxer"
43 German leader after Adenauer
44 Tempur-Pedic alternatives
46 Gut feelings?
47 Actor/comedian ___ Baron Cohen
49 Face-off
52 Shipwreck site, maybe
53 Saltimbocca ingredient
56 Strawberry, raspberry or cherry
58 Inside the box?
59 ___-Cat

by Kameron Austin Collins

ACROSS

1 ___ others
6 Supermarket chain inits.
9 Shortly, for short
13 Part of a fireplace set
14 Onetime court figure
15 Lacking vivacity
16 Classic British rock group
18 Vivacity
19 Pioneering reggae artist whose name is an exclamation
20 Response to an air offensive?
21 Alternative to mushrooms
22 Confused
24 Still has feelings (for)
29 Singer Grande
30 Thanksgiving dinner preference
31 ___ Ren of "Star Wars"
34 Imparts
35 Part of H.R.H.
36 1000 in the military
37 Wise guys?
38 Be sociable
39 Heavenly halo
40 Fruity dessert with a rum-flavored sauce
43 Prime
44 Word that may or may not be a contraction
45 Chihuahua is a Mexican one
46 Attire for some traditional dancing
52 "Me neither"
53 "Bloom County" character whose vocabulary consists mostly of "Thbbft!" and "Ack!"
54 Having moved on from
55 Little creatures recurring in Dalí paintings
56 ___ lines
57 Word that may or may not be a contraction
58 Underground org. in N.Y.C.
59 Famed Miami golf resort

DOWN

1 Feature of Notre-Dame supported by flying buttresses
2 Speck
3 "Enough! I get it!"
4 "99 Luftballons" singer
5 1984 comedy horror film that contributed to the creation of the PG-13 rating
6 Discoveries of Michael Faraday
7 Type-A type
8 Blond in a bar?
9 Spot removers
10 "Hmm . . . all right, I'm in!"
11 Common character in "The Far Side"
12 Make a splash
14 Longstanding disputes
17 Old Testament prophet
20 Chill response
23 Apt ticker symbol for Harley-Davidson
24 Zero on the Beaufort scale
25 Sphere
26 Page seen in a wedding album
27 Michelin offering
28 Echo responder
32 Part of a track
33 Midwest colleague of Representative Ocasio-Cortez
35 Comment that pretends to be subtle, but isn't
36 Structure near a bed?
38 Pasta in a cheesy dish, informally
39 Harpist's home key
41 Hillary Clinton ___ Rodham
42 Perches for houseplants
43 Pilot's place
45 Blanket that won't keep you warm?
47 Big cosmetics chain
48 It's a numbers game
49 Cake topper
50 Hindu deity of virtue
51 Equivalent of "cya" in a text
53 [Just like that!]

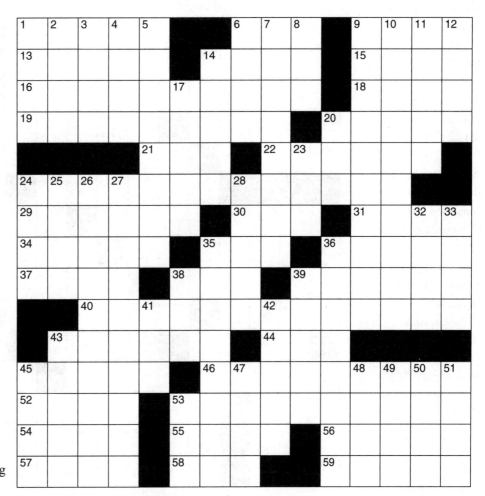

by Robyn Weintraub

ACROSS

1 One who takes stock
12 Can you believe it?!
15 Fear of public places
16 Sticky stuff
17 Tending (to)
18 Half of a frozen foods brand
19 Makes a splash
20 Tapes, say
22 Trees symbolizing death in Celtic culture
23 Crumb
24 Speculative fiction writer Stephenson
25 Go away
27 Before thou knowest
29 Company that owns Rotten Tomatoes
33 Neighbor of Ciudad Juárez
35 On a par with
36 Prepared
37 6–9 months?
38 They're involved in the scheme of things
39 File extensions
40 1986 sci-fi film sequel
42 Pair of skivvies?
44 Writers Patchett and Brashares
45 Tousle
49 Choppered in or out, say
51 Figure that goes through the roof in December?
52 QB's stat: Abbr.
53 Director of two Best Picture-nominated films of the 2010s
55 Issa of comedy
56 "Unforgettable . . . With Love" Grammy recipient
57 Author
58 Lineup on a city block

DOWN

1 Absurdly exaggerated
2 Dexterous
3 As yet
4 Sets off
5 Young woman
6 Brand for determining if you're expecting
7 World's deepest river
8 Survivor at the end of "Hamlet"
9 Long-legged waders
10 Fifth of fünf
11 Steely Dan singer Donald
12 1973 Jim Croce hit
13 Rage quitter, maybe
14 Tavern in the same town as Krusty Burger
21 Leaves home?
23 It bears repeating
25 View from a highland
26 Long-legged waders
28 Communicates nonverbally, in a way
29 Ending with love or snooze
30 Powerful spirits
31 British P.M.'s residence, informally
32 Young woman
34 Things to draw or cast
36 Los Angeles suburb bordering Griffith Park
38 Sticky stuff
41 Not on time for
43 Communicates nonverbally, in a way
45 One of the racing Andrettis
46 Like a prize that's still up for grabs
47 Wooden leg?
48 Venerable advisers
49 Org. whose website has a Social Security Resource Center
50 School house?
51 Tarot reader, e.g.
54 Tweet attachment, at times

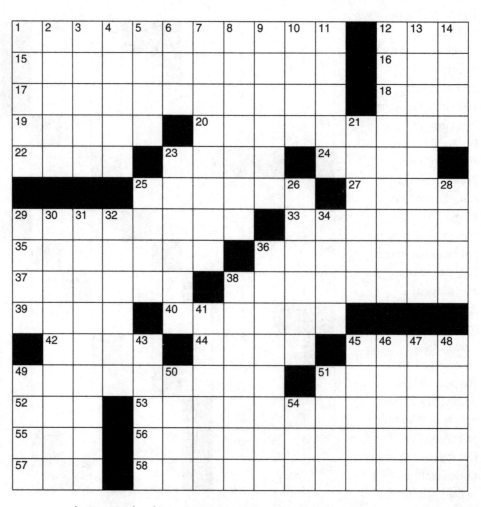

by Patti Varol and Doug Peterson

ACROSS

1 Still on the line, say
5 Slights
10 Big name in razors
14 One of two or three in a typical orchestra
15 Can you believe it?
16 Stuff in a muffin
17 Informal cheer
18 Something about which you might say "It's good!"
20 "Be smart about this, now . . ."
22 It requires some assembly
23 Spiced up
24 Growth ___
26 Actress Rosie of "Do the Right Thing"
29 Shrubland sight
30 Completely off course
35 A home?
38 Without stopping
39 Some early arrivals
41 "Let's go!," in Durango
42 Like some masks
44 Ham it up
45 "Same here"
49 Take part
51 Like some perfume ads
56 Crack jokes, perhaps?
57 Where Jackie Robinson played college ball
58 Northwest county of Pennsylvania
59 Fetal positions?
60 Deck wood
61 One might be pressing
62 Ponders
63 Point on a vane in Spain

DOWN

1 Pulitzer-winning writer Maureen
2 Peek-___
3 Phenomenon discovered by Apollo astronauts
4 Terrarium inhabitant, maybe
5 Take turns, say
6 On deck
7 Feral
8 "Feel the ___" (onetime political slogan)
9 Command that one shouldn't follow
10 Home
11 Goes for it
12 Rushed
13 On edge
19 Fixtures used for pies
21 Penguin's home
24 Store
25 ___ drop (British sweet treat)
27 Big seller of outdoor equipment
28 Suffix with northwest
31 Shortly
32 Cool summer treats
33 Set of awards won by John Legend and Rita Moreno, for short
34 Measurement that might be made in milligrams
36 Zip
37 "To God," in hymns
40 Name on an orange Monopoly property
43 French printmaker ___ Daumier
45 Resort near White River National Forest
46 What two X's make
47 ___ Ziff, antagonist on "The Simpsons"
48 Like unsuccessful chess players
50 Actor Elba
52 Pal
53 Native of Rwanda
54 Unchanged, as on an earnings report
55 Like bot accounts on social media

by Ari Richter

ACROSS

1 Vague sense
5 Nick __, football coach who led both L.S.U. and Alabama to national championships
10 Look out for, say
14 Line outside the entrance?
16 State flower of Utah
17 Using any means necessary
19 The U.S. Open is played on it: Abbr.
20 Supermodel Wek
21 Caesar and others
22 + or −, for a battery
24 Recipe abbr.
26 Torque symbol
27 Kitchen tool for fruit
29 What Neptune's chariot was drawn by
33 Longtime CBS News host Charles
35 Cleared one's cookies?
36 PC program suffix
37 Setting for forensic investigations
41 Bit of needle work
42 Conned
43 Sacked
44 Things typically found in dens
48 Rank
49 "__ et labora" ("Pray and work": Lat.)
50 Like a hoppin' party
51 Target of a 1972 ban
52 Demi of pop
55 Mantel piece
57 "Yo!"
60 Stereotypical cry from a sailor
63 Erin Doherty's role on "The Crown"
64 One involved with an operation
65 Get-up
66 Retreats from the heat
67 Some real heady stuff?

DOWN

1 Mezza __
2 Modern register at a cashless establishment
3 "Let's go!"
4 Pkg. insert
5 Close up
6 Things in the plus column
7 People who might tell you to stop, but probably shouldn't
8 Org. that endorsed Obamacare
9 Court suspensions?
10 Square-cut masonry
11 George Mallory's famous response to "Why did you want to climb Mount Everest?"
12 "Wow!," quaintly
13 Rafts
15 Seasonal seafood delicacy
18 Foe of Caesar
23 Extra-bright
25 Way
27 __ Mesa, Calif.
28 Academy offering
30 Obedience class command
31 Mike Piazza, beginning in 2006
32 Poorly kept
34 Mideast capital
38 Hold for another year, say
39 Censure
40 Way
45 Really fancies
46 Not fancy at all
47 Center of a circle or square, maybe
52 Future D.A.'s hurdle
53 [Gulp!]
54 Thereabouts
56 Some members of the fam
58 Source of the word "trousers"
59 W.W. I battle locale
61 One of the Beastie Boys
62 Fella

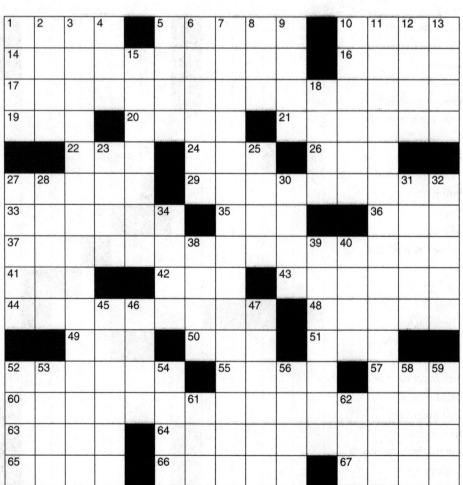

by Damon Gulczynski

ACROSS

1 Temple figure
6 Joins hands?
11 Refresh, as the memory
14 "All this kid stuff now, it's crazy"
15 Fictional hero whose name is Spanish for "fox"
16 Link, of a sort
17 ___ code
18 Setting for the start of "The Sound of Music"
19 Locale traversed by Lewis and Clark: Abbr.
20 Studio upgrade
22 Standouts on the pitcher's mound
23 ___ Bay (place mentioned in "(Sittin' On) The Dock of the Bay")
24 Provides
26 Season ticket holder, presumably
27 Dance traditionally performed to tell a story
30 Reefer
31 Wet-weather footwear
33 Like someone associated with a blue, pink and white flag, for short
34 Time magazine's 2019 Person of the Year
37 Hard to pick up
38 Command after a crash
39 "Sure, that time works for me"
41 Not handle ice well, say
42 Tour grp.
45 Whistle blower
47 Watering hole
49 They end in septembre
50 Type of rental agreement
53 Topper
54 Book club leader on TV
55 Sound
56 "If u ask me . . ."
57 Madame___ (online lifestyle magazine)
58 Pharmaceutical giant, informally
59 Perfect score . . . or half of one
60 Parts of an assembly
61 City NE of Manchester

DOWN

1 Con
2 Supreme Egyptian god
3 Rib-eye request
4 Overindulges in 5-Down
5 Activity by the water cooler
6 Magnate
7 Rebecca in the Basketball Hall of Fame
8 Shaded area
9 Like many biochem majors
10 Kind of flour
11 Spot to pick up a smoothie
12 Process involving a server
13 Readers, e.g.
21 Labor leader?
22 Was su-u-uper into
25 "Better than I expected!"
28 Popular fantasy film franchise, for short
29 Word on either side of "to"
31 Sorting header in a music app
32 "The Avengers" role
34 When the sports preshow ends
35 Used as improv fodder, say
36 Sound
37 Like many a campsite at night
40 Fishing gear left underwater
42 Toy associated with France
43 Throw away all inhibitions
44 Gets to
46 Like ghost stories
48 One of Donald Duck's nephews
51 Major D.C. lobby
52 "___ Gotta Have It"
54 Ending with clip or slip

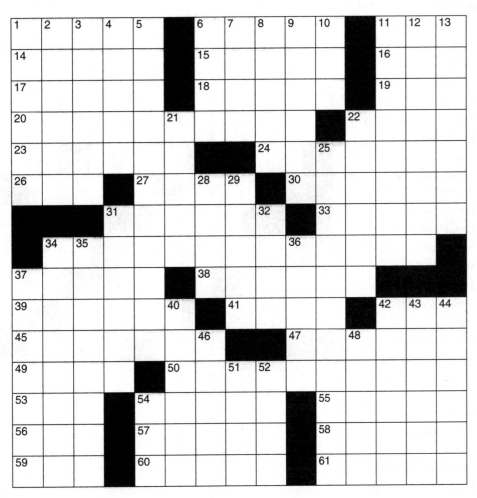

by Erik Agard and Wendy L. Brandes

ACROSS

1 Romania and Bulgaria, once
16 Frank Loesser show tune
17 It might cover an oil spill
18 Doing the rounds?
19 Sporting goods chain with the slogan "Get outside yourself"
20 Potsdam pronoun
21 Peculiar: Prefix
22 Start-up helper: Abbr.
24 Pace at Pompano Park
26 Shoving matches?
29 Relative of une tulipe
31 "Frasier" role
33 Match cry
34 Pooh-pooh
38 "You're probably right"
40 Mojo
41 Sister co. of Virgin
42 Middle square, maybe
43 Sea of __ (view from Crimea's eastern coast)
45 Chart, in Cádiz
48 Sol mates?
50 Frost-covered
52 Crook's place
54 Many activists' concerns: Abbr.
56 One given up for good?
61 "What a sight for sore eyes!"
62 Its islands are not surrounded by water
63 Unease

DOWN

1 Some defensive weapons, in brief
2 "Love and Death on Long Island" novelist Gilbert
3 Lead-tin alloys
4 Unmarried, say
5 Activist Guinier
6 Some claims
7 "Cool, dude"
8 Many a backpacker, at night
9 62-Across option north of the border
10 Go a couple of rounds
11 Preweighed, in a way
12 Very rarely heard instruments
13 Long shift, perhaps
14 Ending to prefer?
15 Young or old follower
23 Rich person's suffix?
25 Alternative to .net
27 Rural parents
28 Cry of pleased surprise
30 Songwriters Hall of Fame member who wrote "April Love"
32 Get-up-and-go
34 Doo-wop syllable
35 Body part detecting odeurs
36 One getting rid of possessions?
37 "Third Watch" actress Texada
39 Hester Prynne wore one
44 Labor Day arrivals, e.g.
46 Conf. whose membership increased by two in 2011
47 Melodic
49 Not leave the house
51 Prefix with second
53 Sticks in the brig?
55 Utah senator who co-sponsored a tariff act
56 Potential serial material
57 "__ in Full" (Tom Wolfe novel)
58 Security figure: Abbr.
59 Abrupt transition
60 Some picnic supplies

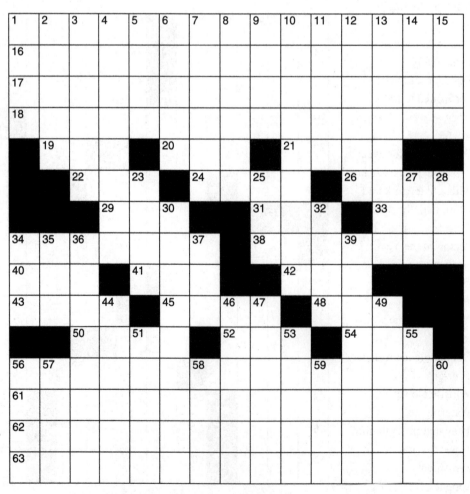

by Martin Ashwood-Smith and Joe Krozel

ACROSS

1 Retreat
9 "3 O'Clock Blues" hitmaker, 1952
15 "Obviously . . ."
16 Uses, as a chaise
17 Particle ejected from an atom during ionization
18 Home of Bwindi Impenetrable National Park
19 "Star Wars" villain name
20 Identify
21 Celebration of the arrival of spring
22 Blew out
24 Eastern hereditary title
26 Specks
27 Things worn at home?
31 Like some details
32 Maddeningly surreal
33 "Girls" home
34 Some adoption candidates
35 Address found online
36 Ones unlikely to drag their feet
38 __ Ruess, lead singer of Fun
39 Weep
40 Order of ancient Greeks
41 There might be a battery of them
42 Rid (of)
43 Matt's onetime "Today" co-host
46 Runs the show, for short
47 Like prosciutto
48 Way over the top
50 Head of the Catholic Church when Luther's "95 Theses" was posted

53 Daddy Warbucks's henchman
54 "Gracious me!"
55 Completely safe, as a proposition
56 Lecture series with well over a billion views

DOWN

1 Century starter?
2 Something in that vein?
3 Line outside a club, maybe
4 Erode
5 Leaves of grass
6 Ran
7 High-level appointee
8 It has all the answers
9 Alternative to cords
10 Bowls, e.g.
11 Mauna __
12 ". . . and who __?"
13 Network connection
14 Part of a moving cloud
20 Foe of the Vikings
22 Tour parts
23 Bigwig
24 High beams
25 Orders in a restaurant
27 Millionaires and billionaires
28 Theodore Roosevelt's domestic program
29 Rapper __ Blow
30 Elite
32 Part of a TV archive

34 Model introduced in the 1990s
37 Target of a 1972 ban
38 "Breakfast at Tiffany's," for one
40 Plain-spoken
42 Took in
43 Routing aid: Abbr.
44 Big Apple neighborhood next to the Bowery
45 "Christians Awake," e.g.
47 Semaphore signals, e.g.
49 Asian path
50 Hog roasting locale
51 Planet whose inhabitants age backward
52 Pair of Dos Equis

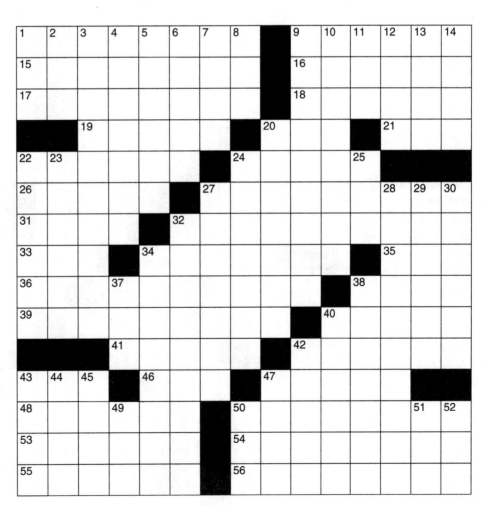

by Peter Wentz

ACROSS

1 "Definitely, dawg!"
10 Art enabled
15 Reading room
16 Timeline segment
17 Reward for knocking 'em dead
18 Moving supply
19 Bare peak
20 Before retitling: Abbr.
21 "It"
22 Drop
24 Name dropper's phrase
26 Cousin of -kin or -let
27 Unpaid babysitters, maybe
29 "Property Virgins" cable channel
30 "Out!"
31 It's often described by horses
33 Regard
34 "And __ the field the road runs by": Tennyson
35 Common loss after a breakup
37 Rush
39 Clipper feature
41 It can be painful to pick up
43 Radio racket
46 Parentheses, e.g.
47 Slight
49 Subject of the 2011 book "The Rogue"
50 Grp. seeking to improve No Child Left Behind
51 "Pensées" philosopher
53 It might mean "hello" or "goodbye" to a driver
54 Woodchuck, e.g.
56 Bradley with five stars
58 Musician who co-founded Nutopia

59 Popular type option
60 "The Pentagon Papers" Emmy nominee
62 Verbal equivalent of a shrug
63 Something awful
64 A couple of rounds in a toaster?
65 Rain forest, e.g.

DOWN

1 Subtle trick
2 Easy chair accompanier
3 Philanthropic mantra
4 Blue symbol of Delaware
5 Prefix with Germanic
6 The Congolese franc replaced it
7 Crest
8 What's often on wheels in an airport
9 Some punk
10 Parts of many chamber groups
11 Pacific port
12 Visually uninspiring
13 15-Across frequenter, maybe
14 "Add __ a tiger's chaudron, / For the ingredients of our cauldron": Shak.
21 "No more guesses?"
23 Blots
25 Astronomical distance: Abbr.
28 It's associated with Chris Rock and 30 Rock

30 Occupy
32 Destroys insidiously
36 Pales
38 More than nod
39 Artificial
40 Relative of a throw
42 Country
44 Hero-worship
45 Learn to teach?
48 Capital on the Niger
51 Some preppy wear
52 Left Turn Only and others
55 A leader and follower?
57 A little blue
60 It can make you squiffy
61 Monopoly quartet: Abbr.

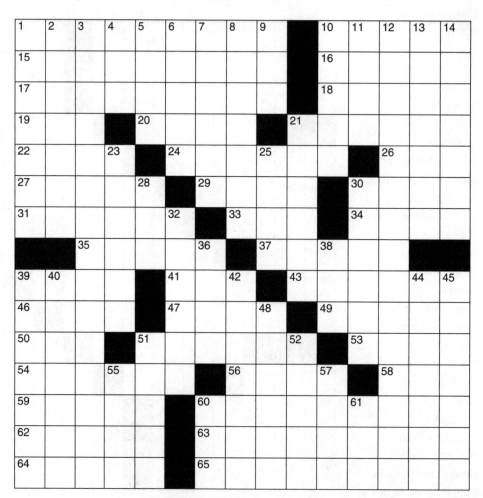

by James Mulhern

ACROSS

1 Take it easy
8 Vostok 1 passenger
15 Try
16 Supermodel Lima
17 Scale with the highest reading at midday, usually
18 More than startle
19 Show horse
20 Juniors' juniors, briefly
22 Those, to José
23 Organ part
25 Classic Jaguar
26 Latin word in legal briefs
27 Princess Leia was one in "A New Hope"
30 Bamboozled
32 It's nothing new
35 Hot shot?
37 Germany, to Britain
39 It helps you focus
40 Unlocked area?
42 Expenditure
43 T-shirt sizes, for short
44 Allstate subsidiary
46 One who deals with stress well?
48 Hat, slangily
49 Reuben ingredient, informally
53 Completely dry, as a racetrack
54 Rub it in
56 Org. with the New York Liberty
57 BlackBerry routers
59 "This statement is false," e.g.
61 Strong and regal
62 Elvis hit with a spelled-out title
63 Gallery event
64 Sharp-pointed instruments

DOWN

1 Sucker
2 Where French ships dock
3 Like many academic halls
4 Help
5 "Cupid is a knavish __": "A Midsummer Night's Dream"
6 Biographical data
7 Love letters
8 One foraging
9 Drinks stirred in pitchers
10 [Back off!]
11 Put on
12 Complain loudly
13 Obsessive need to check one's email or Facebook, say
14 Cons
21 UPS cargo: Abbr.
24 Tennis smash?
26 Puzzle solver's complaint
28 Punishment, metaphorically
29 Hypothetical particle in cold dark matter
31 Turn down
32 Five-time U.S. presidential candidate in the early 1900s
33 School handout
34 Colorful party intoxicant
36 Shrill howl
38 "Just wait . . ."
41 Cream, for example
45 Changes for the big screen
47 Short jackets
50 "Watch __ amazed" (magician's phrase)
51 It takes two nuts
52 Campaign issue
53 Nike rival
54 Mil. bigwig
55 Like sour grapes
58 Long in Hollywood
60 __ Halladay, two-time Cy Young Award winner

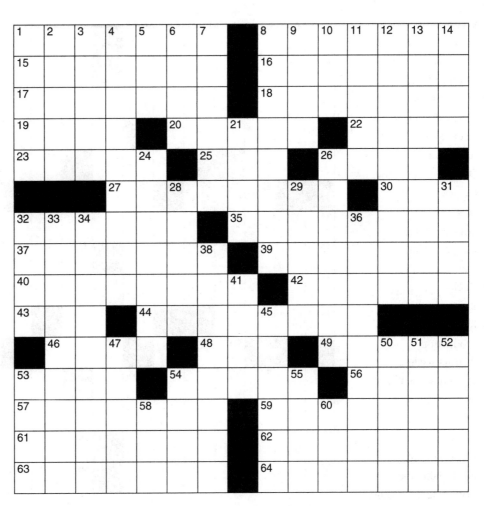

by Joel Fagliano

ACROSS

1 Singer's tongue
8 Fast delivery
15 First name in online news
16 Detox, say
17 Autobiographical book by Carrie Fisher
19 As one
20 D.M.V. offerings
21 Peace Nobelist Kim ——-jung
22 Crispy Twister offerer
24 Peace Nobelist Hammarskjöld
25 Papua New Guinea port in W.W. II news
28 "That's nice"
30 Dept. of Labor division
34 Unit of online popularity
39 "Almost there!"
40 Nice thing to hit
41 First card played in the game parliament
43 British submachine gun
44 Bog
45 Grade sch. class
46 Badge holder: Abbr.
49 Back
51 Ermine, e.g.
54 Kind of cable in TV production
58 Actress Ryder
61 Oscar-nominated Woody Allen film
63 Mythological sister of 66-Across
64 Regardless of
65 Formidable foes
66 Mythological brother of 63-Across

DOWN

1 Went off course, as a ship
2 One of Chekhov's "Three Sisters"
3 Not accept
4 Children's author who created Miss Trunchbull
5 Scoop contents
6 Approached slyly, with "up"
7 1968 space movie villain
8 D. W. Griffith's "—— for Help"
9 "Yeah, you got me"
10 ——-car
11 Fulfill
12 Spanish liqueur
13 "——it?"
14 Staying power
18 Cappuccino choice
23 Not soon at all
26 Who's there
27 ——blue (color named for a school)
29 ——for the best
31 Be hanged after a crime
32 Throng
33 Fine things?
34 Chuck
35 N.Y.C.'s PBS station
36 Big head
37 A.L. West team, on scoreboards
38 ——disease
42 Passed out
47 Stage directions
48 Feline in un jardin zoologique
50 Major League Baseball V.I.P.
52 Merge
53 Demolishes, in Devon
54 Govt. gangbusters
55 Put out
56 Ditto, in footnotes
57 Pupil reactions
59 ——dixit
60 Short breaks, of a sort
62 It may be said with a raised hand

by David Kwong

ACROSS

1 Finish differently, say
8 1950s backup group with four top 10 hits
14 Stars are recognized with them
17 Clear as mud, so to speak
18 It may have pop-ups
19 Scott who co-starred on TV's "Men of a Certain Age"
20 "Incredible!"
21 Not just surmise
23 Closest to zero
24 Years, in Tours
26 Oakland daily, for short
28 "Unfortunately . . ."
29 Deutschland "de"
31 Phoenix setting: Abbr.
33 D.C. nine
35 It has short shortstops
41 "What, no more?"
42 Places for a 35-Across
43 ——other (matchlessly)
44 Satyajit Ray's "The —— Trilogy"
45 Bill in a bow tie
46 Tarantula hawk, e.g.
49 Band options
51 DreamWorks ——
53 Phoenix setting?
55 Jacuzzi session
57 "——of Varnish" (C. P. Snow novel)
61 Chemistry test topic
63 Cursorily
65 Certain Mexican-American
66 Where to come to grips with things?
67 Tight
68 Purports

DOWN

1 Looking up
2 This, in Tijuana
3 Trash hauler
4 Much-filmed swinger
5 Ancient Dravidian's displacer
6 Like Chopin's Mazurka Op. 56 No. 1
7 Sony Reader competitor
8 Middle ear?
9 It's often set in a ring
10 Serve well in court
11 Come to
12 Hometown of the band Hanson
13 Party prizes?
15 "Shh! It's a secret!"
16 Hershey bar
22 Brogue feature
25 "The Moldau" composer
27 Mies van der Rohe was its last director
29 Something needing a stamp
30 Giant giant's family
32 "Giant" events
34 Be overrun
35 Party label for Brit. P.M. William Gladstone
36 Culture centers?
37 Chuck Schumer's predecessor in the Senate
38 Kids' rhyme starter
39 Congress person
40 Works for an editor: Abbr.
46 Takes orders, say
47 Concern of I.R.S. Form 8594
48 Japanese sliding door
50 Head makeup
52 Superman's name on Krypton
54 Hong Kong's Hang —— Index
56 Polynesian drink
58 Pull felt on Earth
59 Part of a French play
60 Cher's role in "Burlesque"
62 "The Natural" hero Hobbs
64 Former Mets manager Hodges

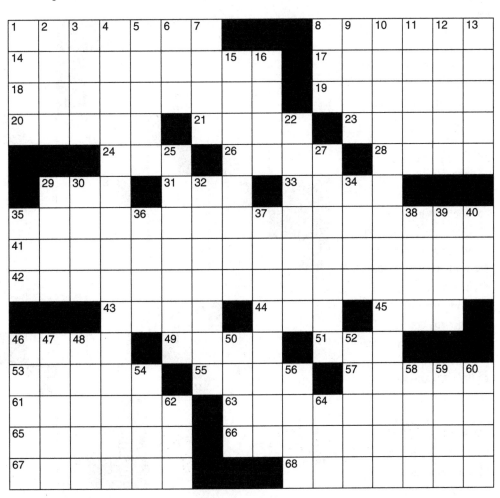

by Derek Bowman

ACROSS

1 Closer to the edge, say
8 Brothers' keepers?
14 Summer time eponym
16 Peso : Mexico :: —— : Panama
17 "NYC 22" replaced it in 2012
18 Key represented by all white keys on a piano
19 Plate holder
20 Kin of clubs
22 Sporty Spice, by another name
23 Hernando's "Hey!"
24 Batcave, e.g.
25 End point of a common journey
26 Ginnie ——
28 Darling
30 Univ. figures
31 Style of New York's Sony Building
34 '60s film character wearing one black glove
35 Literary classic featuring the teen Tadzio
36 Teen "Whoa!"
37 Grp. concerned with violence levels
38 With 43-Across, part of a squid
39 Long-running Mell Lazarus comic strip
41 What you may squeal with
43 See 38-Across
46 "Think of —— . . ."
47 Dipped
48 Biblical waste?
50 Run one's mouth
52 Allowing no equivocation
54 Stupefying thing
55 Favor doer's comment
56 It can be dangerous when leaked
57 Like some sunbathers

DOWN

1 Tree with large seedpods on its trunk
2 Like many older Americans' French or Spanish
3 Not given to lumbering
4 Jacob ——, South African president beginning in 2009
5 Member of the Ennead
6 Attic character
7 Movement from Cuba?
8 Brass tacks
9 Sock sound
10 Bad attribution
11 Aim
12 Where to find some nuts
13 "My heart bleeds for you," often
15 It's known for its start-ups
21 Proceed wearily
24 Unleash
25 "The Once and Future King" figure
26 Extremely
27 Albuterol alleviates it
29 Like some Beanie Babies
31 Sensible
32 Head
33 Groove on an arrow
34 Mailing to a label
35 Pie-baking giant
40 Antares or Proxima Centauri
42 Poet who wrote "Do I dare / Disturb the universe?"
43 Yes or no follower
44 Focus of stereochemistry
45 Roman Demeter
47 Neckline?
48 Union ——
49 Baby sound
51 Verano, across the Pyrenees
53 Yours, in Turin

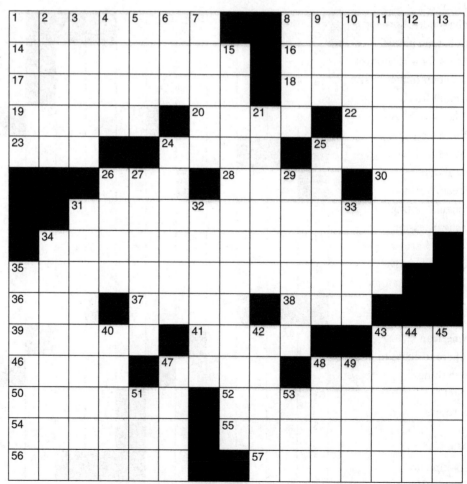

by Josh Knapp

ACROSS

1 Comparable in extent
6 Old White House inits.
9 Convertible setting
14 Holdings
15 "Look at that!"
16 Laughing ——
17 Is curious about
20 N.Y.C. line
21 Some bulls
22 Stranded message?
23 Place to hang something
24 Off-putting?
28 Museum funding org.
29 Scale markings: Abbr.
30 Pajama-clad exec
31 It may help you get from E to F
37 Word with place or prayer
38 Stretch (out)
39 Besmirch
40 Long time
41 Bad quality for dangerous work
45 Put away
46 Google finding
47 Cool
48 Barely lost
54 H.S. subj.
55 Rocky mount
56 ——o menos (basically, in Spanish)
57 Pooh pal
58 Drug study data
62 '90s soccer great Lalas
63 Prince Valiant's son
64 Onetime big name in daytime talk
65 Georges who wrote "Life: A User's Manual"
66 See 67-Across
67 With 66-Across, little source of carbs

DOWN

1 "—— of fools sailing on" (Wang Chung lyric)
2 1998's ——Report
3 Notorious 1960s figure
4 Pension supplement, for short
5 Company of which Thomas Edison was once a director
6 Greets with a beep
7 One perhaps having one too many
8 Doctoral candidate's starting point
9 Large portion of Africa
10 Cries of despair
11 Source of hardwood?
12 18-Down, for one
13 Consumer products firm since 1837, informally
18 Dockworker's grp.
19 Infomercial pioneer Popeil
25 Fig. at the top of an organizational chart
26 Lao-——
27 Asian holiday
31 Big maker of S.U.V.'s
32 Moody's rating
33 Presidential nickname
34 It may be clicked on a computer
35 Cargo on the Spanish Main
36 Grandmother, to Brits
42 Fraternity letter
43 Start of a cheer
44 Japanese computer giant
48 Draw on again
49 Tropical lizard
50 Mauna ——
51 Mineo of movies
52 "I'm serious!"
53 Nurse, at times
59 Computer file suffix
60 ——-Magnon
61 Intl. broadcaster

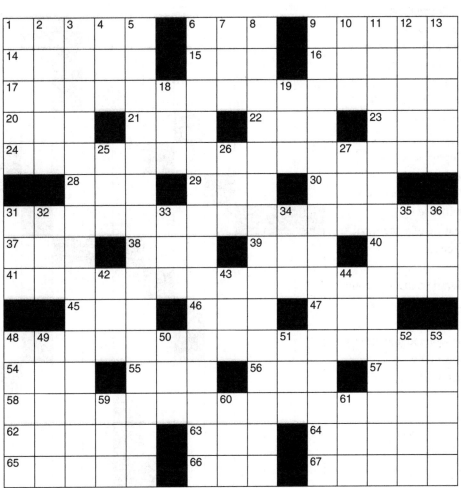

by Joe Krozel

ACROSS

1 "You doubt me?"
9 "Titus" director Taymor
14 Disappointing screen message
15 Series of movements
16 Start of a court display
17 Commensurate (with)
18 What we may be overseas?
19 Relative of a bathysphere
21 Limp Bizkit frontman Fred
23 Ingredient in some pastitsio
24 Sacha Baron Cohen character
25 Football stat.
26 21, in blackjack
28 Have words (with)
29 Earl of Sandwich, e.g.
30 What was once yours?
31 Some charge cards, informally
34 Wee
35 Florentine tourist attraction
36 Certainly didn't roar
39 Bellicose figure
40 Feature of a daredevil circus act
41 Dirt collector
44 Guinness measurement
45 Kool & the Gang's "Get Down ——"
46 Unsolicited manuscripts, informally
48 Get off the ground
51 Instruction for a violinist
52 It follows a curtain opening
53 Hood's support
55 Stir
56 Breather?
57 Gretzky, for most of the 1980s
58 Manages

DOWN

1 Big to-do, maybe?
2 Push to the limit
3 "That cuts me to the quick"
4 Houdini's real name
5 Take the money and run?
6 J. M. W. Turner's "——Banished From Rome"
7 YouTuber, e.g.
8 It keeps people grounded
9 "Fear of Flying" author
10 Brazen
11 Accessory to a suit
12 Many early 20th-century U.S. immigrants
13 Blend with bergamot
15 ——-law
20 Gossip column subject
22 Not live
27 Function of mathematics: Abbr.
29 It's a living thing
30 Much of the Disney Channel's demographic
31 Gets comfortable with
32 Style played on a guitarrón
33 State of stability
34 Shout repeated at a basketball game
36 ——-pedi
37 Causes of head-scratching
38 Hush-hush
40 Farrell of "In Bruges"
41 Hushed sound
42 Get high
43 Strings along a beach?
47 1972 hit that begins "What'll you do when you get lonely . . . ?"
49 "——leads to anger, anger leads to hate, hate leads to suffering": Yoda
50 "You have a point"
54 Naked

by Josh Knapp

ACROSS

1 Dupe
8 Like many PDFs
15 Red-hot
16 Letter
17 Salvage a bad situation
19 Hungarian city known for "Bull's Blood" wine
20 One catching the game
21 Two-time Best Rock Album Grammy winner
22 Acted like a sponge
24 Neighbor of Hercules
25 Critical hosp. setting
26 Founding member of the Star Alliance, for short
27 Automaker Adam
30 Mole removal option
32 Goth relative
33 "——Bein' Bad" (Sawyer Brown country hit)
36 25-Across sights
37 Flipped out
40 Swinging halter, for short
41 Almost fall
42 Last item bagged, often: Abbr.
45 Milling byproducts
47 "——Plays Monterey" (posthumous 1986 album)
48 Chairman —— (hoops nickname)
49 1958–61 polit. alliance
50 Roger Staubach's sch.
53 Home of Sinbad the sailor
55 "Idol ——" (Mozart aria)
56 Cold war weapon?
59 Sorority letters
60 Too pooped to pop
63 Mathematical physicist Roger
64 Assorted
65 Have meals delivered
66 Like some tea

DOWN

1 Mature
2 Antes up for peanuts?
3 Open house invitation
4 Rear admiral's rear
5 Iguana, maybe
6 Music to a masseur's ears
7 Troglodytes troglodytes
8 Grinding material
9 Jack Benny persona
10 Like some giants and dwarfs
11 Prefix with kinetic
12 Why "there's no time for fussing and fighting," per a Beatles hit
13 Shows that one has
14 GPS button
18 Go for broke
23 Kind of beef
28 Fresh
29 Couch attachment?
31 2008 TARP recipient
34 Humanoid cryptid
35 Feel
38 Part of many a German name
39 Smidgen
40 It shows small parts of the picture
43 Whoop it up
44 Like many newlyweds and bagels
45 "Leatherstocking Tales" hero
46 One may give a ring
51 "My bad, Mario!"
52 Spiff (up), in dialect
54 See 62-Down
57 Some indicator lamps, briefly
58 "The Little Mermaid" prince
61 Post-hurricane handout, for short
62 With 54-Down, Best Supporting Actress nominee for 1945's "Mildred Pierce"

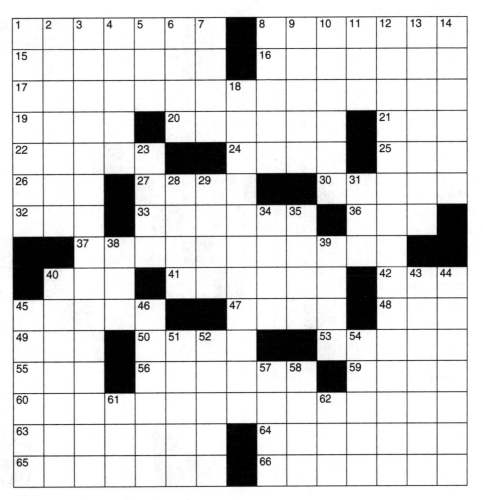

by Ed Sessa

ACROSS

1 Low interest indicator
5 Stick
9 "Debts and —— are generally mixed together": Rabelais
13 Give a second hearing?
14 Go places
15 Buffet table utensil
16 His death prompted Georges Pompidou to say "France is a widow"
19 Show stopper
20 Church cry
21 Spoke lovingly
22 Vegas casino that hosts the World Series of Poker, with "the"
23 Celebrated racehorse nicknamed "The Red Terror"
25 Furniture usually with pillows
28 Hangs on
29 Surfing area?
31 Light weapon
32 Uppercut targets
33 Pier 1 furniture material
34 Not looking 100% well
35 Bad, for good
36 Singer Taylor
37 Notwithstanding
39 Soft lens's makeup
40 Jewelry chain
41 Ultimate problem solver
45 Words after "Oh well"
48 Loaded roll
49 They rate high on the Beaufort scale
50 Pot addition
51 Terminus of the old Virginia and Truckee Railroad
52 Ziploc competitor
53 They're often bagged
54 "This is quite a surprise!"

DOWN

1 Less polite way of saying "no thanks" to offered food
2 Evidence of an allergic reaction
3 Collides with noisily
4 1979 film based on the life of Crystal Lee Sutton
5 Pink fuel
6 Opera with the aria "Recondita armonia"
7 Volkswagen subsidiary
8 Getting through
9 Daphne, after her mythical transformation
10 Wasted, as time
11 "Phantom Lady" co-star Raines
12 Go for
15 Exerts oneself
17 Survivor of two 1918 assassination attempts
18 Rejoices tactlessly
23 "The American Crisis" pamphleteer
24 One of the Colonial Colleges, informally
25 Ground water?
26 Paperless way to read the paper
27 Only founding member of OPEC not located in the Mideast
28 "Come again?"
30 Wax worker
32 Ad agency acquisition
33 Fried appetizer
35 Flares
36 Summer Triangle star
38 Not to be disrespected
39 River mentioned in the Rig Veda
41 Historic caravel
42 Bar rooms?
43 Tennis's Dementieva
44 Many a filling material
45 One with a job opening?
46 Like the leaves of a trailing arbutus
47 Robert Louis Stevenson described it as "bottled poetry"

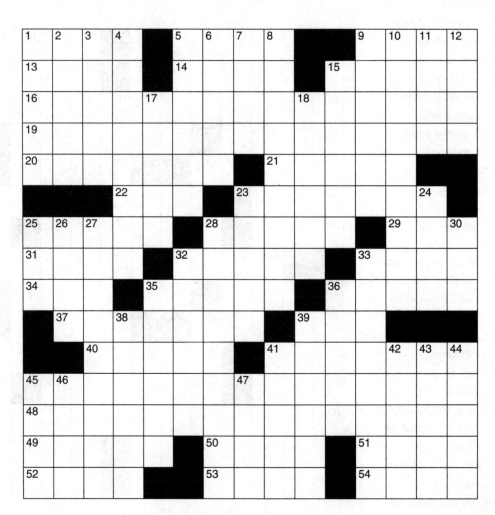

by Patrick Berry

ACROSS

1 Dinner spread
11 Streets of Rage maker
15 Gardening brand
16 Roman 18-Across
17 Former "Weekend Update" host on "S.N.L."
18 Greek 16-Across
19 Three-time All-Star pitcher Robb
20 Karnak Temple deity
22 Airport on Flushing Bay, in brief
23 "My Baby No —— Aqui" (Garth Brooks song)
25 Family head
26 When the French celebrate Labor Day
27 Box fillers
30 Line to Wall Street, for short
31 N.B.A.'s Magic, on sports tickers
32 Responded to a dentist's request
33 Emblem
35 ——failure
36 Critic Ebert, informally
37 Element with a low atomic number that is not found naturally on Earth
38 They cross many valleys
40 Gracefully quit
41 Time gap
42 Chris with the 1978 hit "Fool (If You Think It's Over)"
43 Antiquity
44 ——glance
45 Its first complete ed. was published in 1928
46 Is worthwhile
47 0
48 Hot
50 T.A.'s pursuit, maybe
53 "Sure ——!"
55 Ruin the surprise, perhaps
58 Gadget's rank in cartoons: Abbr.
59 On- and off-road
60 Cruising
61 Movie mogul whom Forbes magazine once named the highest-paid man in entertainment

DOWN

1 Fed concerned with forgery
2 "Paris, Je T'——" (2006 film)
3 Leader in women's education?
4 Sitting formation
5 Prefix with sphere
6 Slip-preventing, in a way
7 ——Brothers
8 View lasciviously
9 Hot
10 "Ye gods!"
11 Kind of request in a Robert Burns poem
12 N.B.A. Hall-of-Famer who, with Walt Frazier, formed the Knicks' "Rolls Royce Backcourt"
13 Outgoing
14 Hit makers, say
21 Bacterium binder
23 Old lab burners
24 Common sushi garnish
27 TV sketch comedy set in the "city where young people go to retire"
28 They're ordered by mathematicians
29 Some French-speaking Africans
33 Apple's mobile/tablet devices run on it
34 Red-carpet interview topics
36 Like some files
39 Views lasciviously
40 "Bigger & ——," 1999 Grammy-winning comedy album by Chris Rock
43 It's a downer
49 Giveaway
50 Jelly Belly flavor
51 Willing participant?
52 Fashion company with a Big Apple flagship store
54 Thermal ——
56 Calder contemporary
57 Historic beginning?

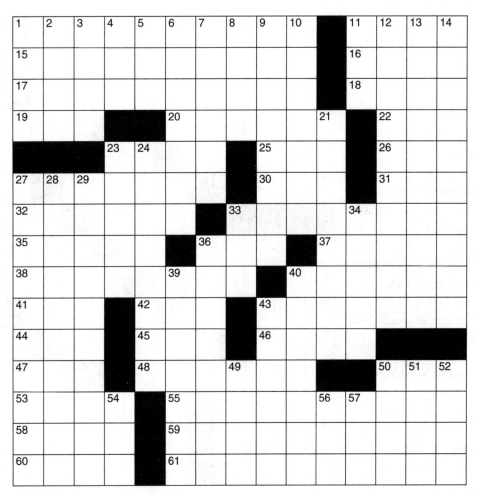

by Michael Sharp

ACROSS

1 Mobile home?
11 Made fun of, in a way
15 Bygone sportscaster with a statue outside Wrigley Field
16 Fan letters?
17 They may lead to another story
18 "Popular Fallacies" byline, 1826
19 Not so apple-cheeked
20 "Sure, I'm game"
22 Overzealous promgoer's choice, maybe
23 Address add-on
25 Noted press conference rhymer
26 What some swatches preview
27 Where Achilles was dipped to make him invincible
28 Represener of time, often
30 Part of a publicity agent's job
31 Ochoa who was the first #1-ranked golfer from Mexico
32 Waltz component
36 O, more formally
37 Fee on some out-of-state purchases
38 Bats
39 Longtime Capone rival
40 Lodging for a night out?
41 Single mom in a 2000s sitcom
45 Party to the Oslo Accords, for short
46 In the loop, with "in"
48 South Pacific palm
49 Business that may be a zoning target
51 Walk ostentatiously
52 Drop
53 Some contemporary ads
56 Chance upon
57 Unlikely pageant winners
58 Muddles
59 Many a John Wayne pic

DOWN

1 Scabbard
2 Base for Blackbeard
3 Fictional student at Riverdale High
4 Train track parts
5 Actors Talbot and Waggoner
6 Disney villain
7 Monopoly token
8 Spanish occupational suffix
9 Pitch producer
10 Dissolved, as bacteria exposed to antibodies
11 "Double" or "triple" move
12 Certain medieval combatant
13 Rhett Butler's "Frankly, my dear, I don't give a damn," e.g.
14 Nanny's order
21 State with Leipzig and Dresden
23 Stick in a cabinet
24 Objectivist Rand
27 X-ray ——
29 Chihuahua cry
30 Stop
31 What a brush may pick up
32 Ices
33 Common number of gondoliers
34 Intern's duty, maybe
35 Stop: Abbr.
36 Magician's prop
38 Lightning bolt shape
40 Mississippi site of Machine Gun Kelly's last known bank robbery
41 Close again, as a change purse
42 Emission of ripening fruit
43 Ending with flag or pall
44 Actress Milano of "Charmed"
47 Marked acidity
48 Earl Scruggs's instrument
50 The E.P.A. issues them: Abbr.
51 Cogent
54 Dial unit
55 "Encore!," to a diva

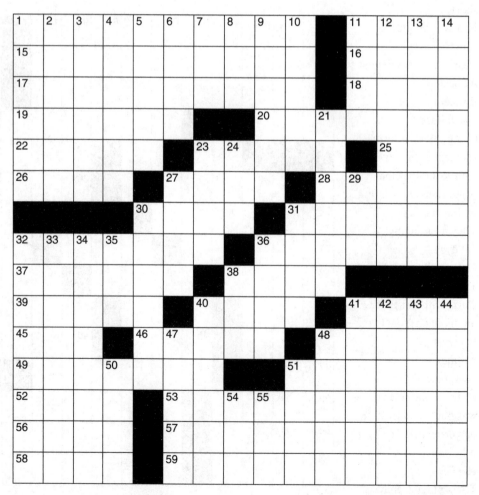

by Ian Livengood and Brad Wilber

ACROSS

1 Utah's —— Range
8 Snatches
15 Where to check for prints?
16 Kind of pie
17 What a blog provides
18 Cornish knight of the Round Table
19 Bud of Nancy
20 "Ghost" character Brown
22 The working girl in "Working Girl"
23 Euro dispenser
25 Freshwater predator
26 Semester, e.g.
27 "That —— stupid!"
28 Richard Gere title role
29 Addresses shrilly
31 1980s TV outfit
34 "Am —— blame?"
35 Date shown on the tablet of the Statue of Liberty
39 Blood-typing system
40 Converses
41 Situated near the middle line of the body
43 Formed a junction
44 Itinerant people of Europe
48 $2 to $2,000, in Monopoly
49 Actor Hamm of "Mad Men"
50 "The accuser of our brethren," per Revelation
51 Digital imaging brand
52 ——oil
54 Port vessel
55 University of Cincinnati athlete
57 Former Colts arena
59 Bend backward
60 J, F or K
61 Turner backers
62 Scale often used in a laboratory

DOWN

1 Condiment that can make your eyes water
2 Coffee and fresh-baked cookies have them
3 Adds color to
4 "Antony and Cleopatra" prop
5 Banned
6 Lug
7 "I Ching" figures
8 Orange dwarf
9 German possessive pronoun
10 "——ever!"
11 Jet wing warning
12 When to wear a cocktail dress, traditionally
13 Sports bar feature
14 Aid and abet: Abbr.
21 Oscar winner once named Sexiest Man Alive by People
24 20th-century French leader
26 Record label for the Miracles and Stevie Wonder
28 Massachusetts governor ——Patrick
29 Entry in a celebrated international sports competition since 1851
30 French pronoun
32 Drum kit part
33 Odd
35 Preserves, perhaps
36 Epithet for a computer whiz
37 Eat crow
38 Bonus, in ads
42 Mired
45 Holy Roman emperor known as "the Red"
46 Fighters for Kenyan independence
47 Little dears
49 Early invaders of Britain
50 Slow racer
51 Shelter dug into a hillside
52 Pitching stat
53 Middle school marks?
56 Monitor, for short
58 Shakes

by Paula Gamache

ACROSS

1 "Not much at all for me, please"
10 Bare
15 Director Michelangelo
16 Big name in movie theaters
17 What gets the shaft?
18 Struck, as by God
19 *Basketball area
20 Unlike Iago
22 *100%
23 Not run, maybe
25 Co. that introduced Dungeons & Dragons
26 Cane material
28 Abhorrent
30 Symbol of modesty
32 *Water cooler
33 British critic Kenneth who created "Oh! Calcutta!"
34 Women, old-fashionedly
36 Bit of flimflam
38 Third-place candidate in the 1920 presidential election who ran his campaign from jail
39 Skiing mecca
43 *Submerged
47 Outwits
48 Alternative indicator
49 Ageless, in an earlier age
50 Portmanteau food brand
52 Microscopic messenger
54 Sets (on)
55 *Had charges
56 Pizarro contemporary
59 Cousin of a cistern
60 Messed (with)
62 Many British mathematicians
64 Came (from)
65 So that one might
66 Wood fasteners
67 Revolutionary invention for restaurants?

DOWN

1 Something good to hit
2 Asleep, say
3 What an agoraphobe does
4 Big load
5 Symbol of life
6 Daisies and the like, botanically
7 Stable colors
8 Even or close to even, in a tennis set
9 Circlegraph shapes
10 '14s in '14, e.g.
11 Lead on
12 Relatives of guinea pigs
13 Grind
14 Product that might be used with a blessing
21 Like "Have a nice day," for example
24 Takes off
27 Nearly
29 Left over
31 ——of the earth
34 Gets set
35 Feudal thralls
37 Table leaves?
39 Target, in a way
40 Like Europe in 1945
41 Cry in hide-and-seek
42 Image
44 Those who should follow the advice in the sounded-out answers to the five starred clues
45 Wikipedia precursor
46 Uses for support
49 Grill, e.g.
51 Words of explanation
53 Cramming aid
57 ——Zátopek, four-time Olympic track gold medalist
58 Delta 88, e.g., informally
61 Paris's Avenue —— Champs-Élysées
63 Money of Romania

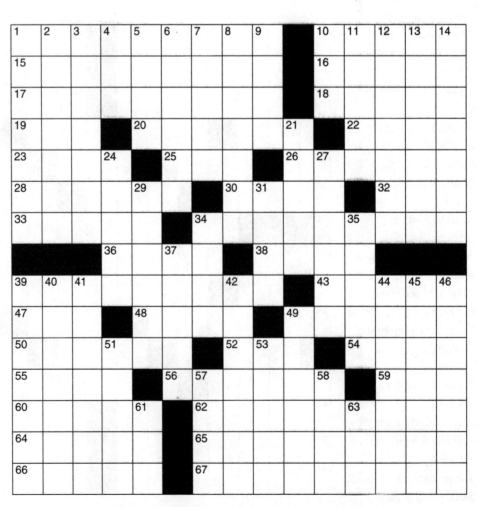

by Matt Ginsberg

ACROSS

1 Winning smile, e.g.
6 International cricket event
15 Too-familiar
16 Road built during the Samnite Wars
17 Press conference segment
18 Game ender, possibly
19 Working for
20 Republican who won Bentsen's vacated Senate seat
21 Band with a person's name
23 1970 Kinks album title starter
24 Afternoon reception
25 Orange growers
26 Joe who was retired in 1997
27 Folk medicine plant
29 Music genre prefix
30 Clears the mind, with "up"
31 Chow
33 Chase off
34 "Things Fall Apart" novelist
37 Escort, as to the door
38 What the name "Rhoda" means
42 Trying minors
43 What repellent might prevent
45 New Deal program, for short
46 Heady feeling
47 She and Clark Gable were known as "the team that generates steam"
49 Surrounded with foliage
51 Impressive, as accommodations
52 Player of Sal in "The Godfather"
53 Call to mind
54 "Don't decide right away"
55 Parties with mai tais, maybe
56 Titan's home
57 Shrill cries

DOWN

1 British P.M. when W.W. I began
2 One who's unseated?
3 Land line?
4 Tribal bigwig
5 Claw
6 Five-time N.C.A.A. basketball champs from the A.C.C.
7 Uniform ornament
8 Thwarts for petty reasons
9 Add color to
10 1968 novel set in Korea
11 Opposed to the union, say
12 Couple
13 Performer on the road?
14 Note books used in church?
22 Stevedore's burden
26 Gentle murmur
28 "Music should strike fire from the heart of man, and bring tears from the eyes of woman" speaker
30 Undercover item?
32 Exercise target
33 Begin planning the nuptials
34 Way to walk while conversing
35 Fall apart
36 Fallen star
37 How Congress might adjourn
39 Major error in soccer
40 "Louder!"
41 Seal classification
43 Magna Carta's drafters
44 Without doubt
47 Largely hollow bricks
48 Flo Ziegfeld offering
50 Erase

by Patrick Berry

ACROSS

1 First rock band whose members received Kennedy Center Honors
7 Jiffy
11 Shade of black
14 Fix, in carpentry
15 Undoubtedly
17 Dropped a line?
18 Olympians' food
19 Figures for investors
20 Animal that catches fish with its forepaws
21 Ward on a set
22 Shade of gray
24 Work __
25 Annual with deep-pink flowers
28 Miles off
30 Tailor
33 Part of the Dept. of Labor
34 All-Star Martinez
35 "Guys and Dolls" composer/lyricist
37 Like dirty clothes, often
39 Secondary: Abbr.
40 The muscle of a muscle car, maybe
42 Soup scoop
43 Fill
44 ABBA's genre
46 "Alice" actress Linda
48 Kyrgyzstan's second-largest city
49 Game discs
53 Uncopiable, say
55 Quick session for a band
57 Springsteen hit with the lyric "Only you can cool my desire"
58 Noted graffiti artist
59 Viking, e.g.
60 Philosophize, say
61 Strike leader?
62 Breather
63 Trained groups

DOWN

1 Sights at the dentist's office
2 Three-time Olympic skating gold medalist
3 Georgia of "The Mary Tyler Moore Show"
4 1955 Pulitzer-winning poet
5 Rushed
6 Maxim
7 Pot and porn magazines, typically
8 Norton Sound city
9 Diplomat who wrote "The Tide of Nationalism"
10 Reform Party founder
11 Legitimate
12 Construction project that began in Rome
13 Rush
16 "Yeah . . . anyway"
23 Ultra sound?
26 Boolean operators
27 Charging things?
29 Ensnare, with "in"
30 "It wasn't meant to be"
31 Literally, "the cottonwoods"
32 Those with will power?
36 Exactly 10 seconds, for the 100-yard dash
38 Spanish greeting
41 Tending to wear away
45 Illogically afraid
47 Draw (from)
50 Actor Werner of "The Spy Who Came in From the Cold"
51 Heroic tale
52 Lid afflictions
53 Cleaner fragrance
54 They're sometimes named after presidents
56 Squat

by Brendan Emmett Quigley

ACROSS

1 Food item resembling an organ
11 Not long-departed
15 Question after a public shellacking
16 Plutoid just beyond the Kuiper Belt
17 Many a detective film cover-up
18 Squire
19 Lack of authorisation?
20 "Casablanca" carrier
22 It really stands out
25 Be loud at a funeral, say
26 Many 56-Across users
29 It may have check marks
30 General exercise?
31 Stretches out
35 "We're in trouble now!"
36 Abbr. on a sports ticker
37 Topics at some religious retreats
41 Cousin of a screwdriver
44 Largest city in the South Pacific
45 Go back on
46 Six bells in the morning watch
49 Prefix with geek
50 Hand picks?
52 Monogram of the author of "A Charge to Keep: My Journey to the White House"
55 Kind of block
56 It replaced the Indian rupee in 1932
60 Winnipeg's __ Franko Museum
61 Ithaca is at its southern end
62 Be inclined
63 His Secret Service code name was Providence

DOWN

1 Classic name in New York delis
2 Subject precursor
3 Like some eggs
4 Intro to Euclidean geometry?
5 Letter abbr.
6 Casual assent
7 As
8 Weena's race, in fiction
9 Generally speaking
10 Big name in video streaming
11 Five and ten, e.g.
12 Ticketmaster info, maybe
13 Coloring
14 Compact first name?
21 Formation on 28-Down
22 About 186,282 miles
23 Marathoner Pippig
24 NASA's Aquarius, e.g.
26 Done some strokes
27 Routine reaction?
28 See 21-Down
32 Home of the Black Mts.
33 Crow relatives
34 Stock mover
38 Shrimp
39 Midas's undoing
40 Katana wielder
41 Curt
42 Beauregard follower
43 GPS abbr.
46 Cheerleader's move
47 Relative d'un étudiant
48 Many an animal rights activist
51 Baseball Hall-of-Famer who played for the Giants
52 Bother, with "at"
53 After-life gathering?
54 Backwoods relative
57 Starting device: Abbr.
58 Code word
59 Publisher of World of Work mag.

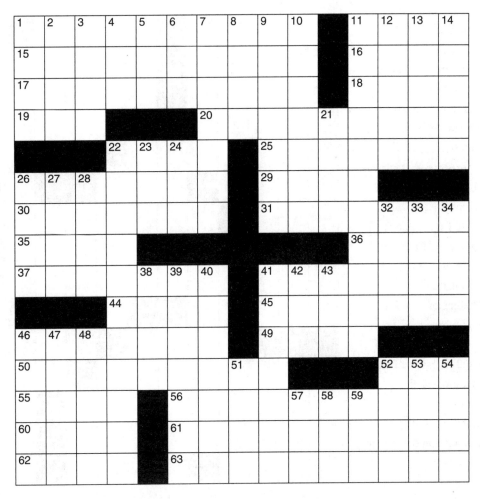

by Barry C. Silk

ACROSS

1 Where Union Pacific is headquartered
6 Chinese __ (popular bonsai trees)
10 Medieval drudge
14 Sister of Castor and Pollux
15 Fighter getting a leg up?
17 Site of Tiberius' Villa Jovis
18 Page on the stage
19 Comfortable
21 Taking place (in)
22 One-point throws
24 Appliance sound
25 Checkers, for instance
26 Play critic?
28 Hype
32 Onetime Arapaho foe
33 Grooming tool
36 Vietnamese holiday
37 O-shaped
38 Priest in I Samuel
39 Dread Zeppelin or the Fab Faux
41 Sports div. that awards the George Halas Trophy
42 Gold Cup venue
43 Quote qualification
44 Coin of many countries
45 Pretension
48 Get more inventory
50 Country whose flag is known as the Saltire
54 Bubble handler?
55 Foundation devoted to good works?
57 Uniform
58 Bag lady?
59 Less often seen
60 Deep black
61 Twist
62 America's Cup trophies, e.g.

DOWN

1 Broadway musical with two exclamation points in its name
2 They might have bones to pick
3 Like characters in a script
4 Some wetlands wildlife
5 Miyazaki film genre
6 Hosp. record
7 Creates an account?
8 Fast-food debut of 1981
9 Go along effortlessly
10 Vending machine drink
11 What to do when you have nothing left to say?
12 Peace Nobelist Cassin
13 Dance-pop trio Right Said __
16 Symbol of happiness
20 Off the mark
23 English Channel feeder
27 Bad line readings
29 Launched the first round
30 Narcissistic one
31 Handheld "Star Trek" devices
33 Sea creature whose name means "sailor"
34 Huxtable family mom
35 Surgical cutter
40 Gondoliers, e.g.
44 Like a poli sci major, maybe
46 Woodworking tools
47 Underhanded schemer
49 American Airlines hub
50 Drink served in a masu
51 Zodiac symbol
52 Palindromic man
53 "My man!"
56 Plaintive pet sound

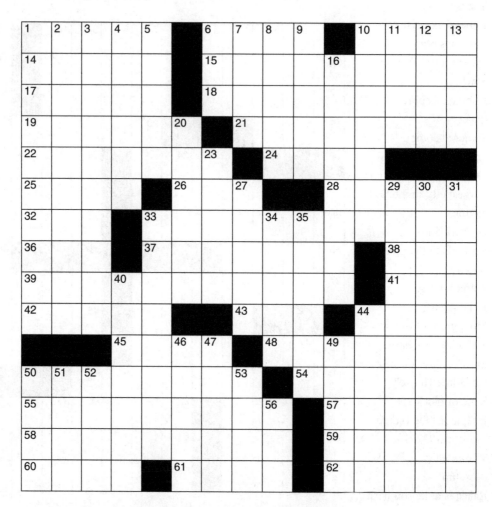

by Patrick Berry

ACROSS

1 Fighting
6 Amscray
10 They get taken easily
14 ___ Road (W.W. II supply route)
15 Hospital bed feature
16 Nail
17 Circular side?
19 Unisex name meaning "born again"
20 Many a security point
21 Straight
23 Form of "sum"
24 Sound name
25 Tom who won a Tony for "The Seven Year Itch"
26 Ones keeping on their toes?
29 The City of a Hundred Spires
31 Triage determination
32 Home of "NerdTV"
35 Line of rulers
37 Big game plans?
39 Argument-ending letters
40 Short distance
42 Occasions for bulldogging
43 Hot-and-cold menu item
45 Mathematician Cantor who founded set theory
48 Going without saying?
49 Aid in getting back on track
52 Means of reducing worker fatigue
54 Kraft Nabisco Championship org.
55 Color also known as endive blue
56 Classic Hitchcock set
58 Quiet place to fish
59 Suffixes of 61-Across
60 Rich of old films
61 Contents of some ledges
62 "___ Wedding" ("The Mary Tyler Moore Show" episode)
63 Occasioned

DOWN

1 Flat, e.g.
2 Fixes flats?
3 Hospital patient's wear
4 See 5-Down
5 With 4-Down, lost control
6 Feature of some western wear
7 Pathfinder?
8 Reagan was seen a lot in them
9 Word after who, what or where, but rarely when
10 Things driven on construction sites
11 Anti-inflammatory product
12 Authorities might sit on one
13 Wonderful
18 Kind of wheel
22 One putting the pedal to the metal
24 Summer symbol?
27 One of the Eastern elite
28 Aviation safety statistic
29 Straightaway
30 Manhattan choice
32 Broken into on TV?
33 Kind of lab
34 Nemesis of some dodgers: Abbr.
36 Fellow chairperson?
38 Use a 24-Down
41 Like pigtails
43 Talks tediously
44 Hacker's achievement
45 American company whose mascot has a Cockney accent
46 Diamond flaw
47 Diagonal rib of a vault
50 One getting cuts
51 Early: Prefix
53 Exit lines?
54 Ethnologist's interest
57 254,000 angstroms

by Dana Motley

ACROSS

1 Human-powered transport
8 Lingerie enhancements
15 Japanese "thanks"
16 Consumed
17 Like some Mideast ideology
18 Grammy-winning singer from Barbados
19 "___ me later"
20 Barrister's deg.
21 Belief opposed by Communists
22 Hammer and sickle
24 Small arms
25 "Be right there"
29 Labor outfits
30 Bubbly brand, for short
34 Oral reports?
35 Des Moines-to-Cedar Rapids dir.
36 It's known to locals as Cymraeg
37 "Money" novelist, 1984
38 Orange entree, informally
40 Not take a back seat to anyone?
41 Diner freebies
45 Fisherman's Wharf attraction
46 Young colleen, across the North Channel
48 Browns' home, for short
49 Bring to a boil?
52 By the boatload
53 Wastes
55 Cubs' home
56 Improbable victory, in slang
57 Potentially embarrassing video
58 Mezzo-soprano Troyanos

DOWN

1 Quebec preceder, to pilots
2 Meaningful stretches
3 Soft touch?
4 Supermarket inits.
5 Some bank offerings
6 Totally flummoxed
7 Spring figure?
8 Pitcher Blyleven with 3,701 strikeouts
9 Oatmeal topping
10 Close
11 Unit of wisdom?
12 "Little Girls" musical
13 Actress Kirsten
14 Hits with some trash
22 Sporty auto options
23 Torch carriers
25 Capital of South Sudan
26 Old one
27 Her voice was first heard in 2011
28 It's already out of the bag
30 Parts of a school athletic calendar
31 Designer Cassini
32 "Mi casa ___ casa"
33 Segue starter
36 Everything, with "the"
38 Trip
39 Fried tortilla dish
40 Landlocked African land
41 Collectors of DNA samples
42 Hides from Indians, maybe?
43 Chill
44 All-points bulletin, e.g.
47 Final word in a holiday tune
49 Locale for many political debates
50 Perdition
51 Site of the Bocca Nuova crater
54 Poli ___

by Ian Livengood

ACROSS

1 First female candidate to win the Ames Straw Poll
16 War paths
17 It airs in the morning, ironically
18 Case builders: Abbr.
19 Copy from a CD
20 Understood
21 Show featuring special agents
22 Red Cloud, e.g.
24 Player of the bad teacher in "Bad Teacher"
26 Rear
27 Possible rank indicator
29 Overseas relig. title
30 Big name in car monitors
32 Beat it
34 "Keep dreaming!"
36 Word after a splat
37 Like some lovers' hearts
41 Strikes
45 She may be fawning
46 Colorful cover-ups
48 Brandy letters
49 Grilling test
51 Misses abroad: Abbr.
52 Newborn abroad
53 ___ Hedin, discoverer of the Trans-Himalaya
55 Folman who directed the 2013 film "The Congress"
56 Comcast Center hoopster
57 Alternative to a breakfast burrito
61 Big source for modern slang
62 Some critical comments from co-workers

DOWN

1 Yellowstone setting: Abbr.
2 Odysseus, e.g.
3 Dopes
4 Knocks off
5 Control tower info
6 Re-serve judgment?
7 Female adviser
8 Ill-humored
9 Norwegian Star port of call
10 Old oscilloscope part, briefly
11 Turns over in one's plot?
12 Was reflective
13 Its adherents are in disbelief
14 Formula one?
15 Neighbor of Victoria: Abbr.
21 Top kick, for one: Abbr.
22 Puck and others
23 Some exact likenesses
25 Part of Queen Elizabeth's makeup?
27 Certain league divisions
28 Forerunners of discs
31 Kind of cross
33 They may be returned with regrets: Abbr.
35 458 Spider and F12 Berlinetta
37 Production
38 Definitely
39 Give some space, say
40 Grind
42 Stormed
43 Modern mouse hole?
44 Ring bearer, maybe
47 Emulates Homer
50 Actor Burton
52 Competitor of Lauren and Klein
54 Numerical prefix
56 First name in footwear
57 "Two, three, four" lead-in
58 Org. with a clenched fist logo
59 Org. created right after the cold war
60 MS-DOS component: Abbr.

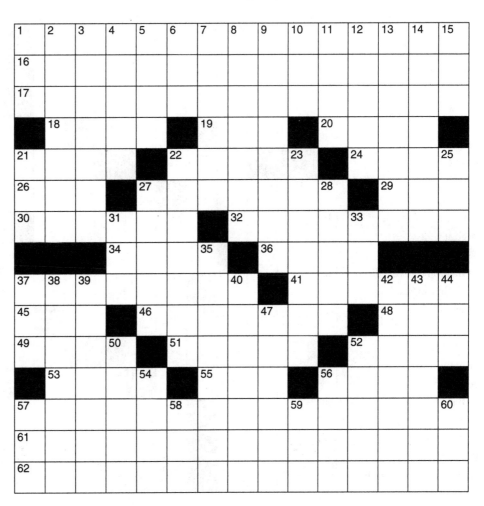

by David Steinberg

40

ACROSS

1 Old Hollywood low-budget studios, collectively
11 "Oh, God!" actress
15 Wine bottle contents in Hitchcock's "Notorious"
16 Only event in which Venezuela medaled at the 2012 Olympics
17 Dessert often with cream cheese icing
18 Ironwoman org.?
19 Singer born Eithne Ní Bhraonáin
20 Map inits. created in the wake of the Suez Crisis
21 Now-rare connection method
23 Blather
25 Big name in markers
26 Nitroglycerin, for one
29 Director's alternative to a dolly
32 It was dissolved in 1991
34 Time in TV ads
35 Fused
36 Fortify
38 Domingo, e.g.
39 Onetime TV music vendor
41 Kind of community
43 Avocado relative
45 Ross Sea sights
46 Interrupts
47 Strike out
48 Excoriates
49 "Revolution 9" collaborator
51 It may slip in the back
55 L.B.J. biographer Robert ___
56 One-third of a triangle, maybe
59 Hindi relative
60 The goddess Kali appeared on its first cover
61 Bygone
62 New Jersey childhood home of Whitney Houston and Queen Latifah

DOWN

1 Brownish purple
2 Port where Camus set "The Plague"
3 Fluctuate
4 Brings to a boil
5 Rock in ___ (major music festival)
6 "Coppélia" attire
7 Hit from the 1978 disco album "Cruisin'"
8 More than chuckle
9 Planet first mentioned on "Happy Days"
10 It's used to define a border
11 Colorful dessert
12 Press production
13 Doing a government agency's job
14 Garner
22 Not the party type?: Abbr.
24 Part of 20-Across
25 Substance that citrus peels are rich in
26 Endor natives
27 Site of the last battle of the Cuban Revolution
28 Barriers used in urban renewal projects
29 Ire
30 Get a hint of
31 Party tray array
33 Vexing
37 Country name
40 Releases
42 Baseball's ___ Line (.200 batting average)
44 Prime meridian std.
47 Skip
48 Smallish lingerie spec
49 Electrical units
50 Ordered
52 "You can count on me"
53 Provided backup, in a way
54 Deep or high lead-in
57 Org. with inspectors
58 "A defeat for humanity," per Pope John Paul II

by Brad Wilber and Doug Peterson

ACROSS

1 Holding
9 Way of looking at things
14 Reading light for an audiobook?
16 Detergent component
17 Going nowhere?
18 Pine for
19 Org. always headed by a U.S. general or admiral
20 Baltic native
22 "After ___"
23 Seat cushions?
25 Old airline name
28 Roofing choice
29 "According to reports . . ."
32 Wedded
33 They make a racket
34 Cell alternatives
35 Like each word from this clue
37 Many a time
40 Change places
41 White spread
42 Heavy and clumsy
43 White of the eye
45 The Dom is the third-highest one
46 A whole bunch
49 Blows a fuse
50 Nation with the most Unesco World Heritage Sites
53 Winner over Ohio State in 1935's so-called "Game of the Century"
55 Suez Crisis setting
56 Startling revelation
57 Xerox competitor
58 Buffalo Bill and Calamity Jane wore them

DOWN

1 Hold firmly, as opinions
2 Stuff used to soften baseball mitts
3 Generally
4 Hill house
5 "A whizzing rocket that would emulate a star," per Wordsworth
6 Big name in storage
7 Boortz of talk radio
8 Swinger?
9 Diane Sawyer's employer
10 Land on the Arctic Cir.
11 Most dismal
12 Mouthwash with the patented ingredient Zantrate
13 Shakespearean stage direction
15 Depression creator
21 Crab apple's quality
24 Old-fashioned respirator
26 Not as outgoing
27 Communist bloc news source
30 Experienced
31 Fountain drinks
33 Wrist bones
34 Lamebrain
35 It's not fair
36 Car collectors?
37 Greek salad ingredient
38 They arrive by the truckload
39 Movie trailers, e.g.
40 Carriage with a folding hood
41 Turbine parts
44 Advanced slowly
47 School door sign
48 Amendment to an amendment
51 Southeast Asian language
52 Dark side
54 Ikura or tobiko

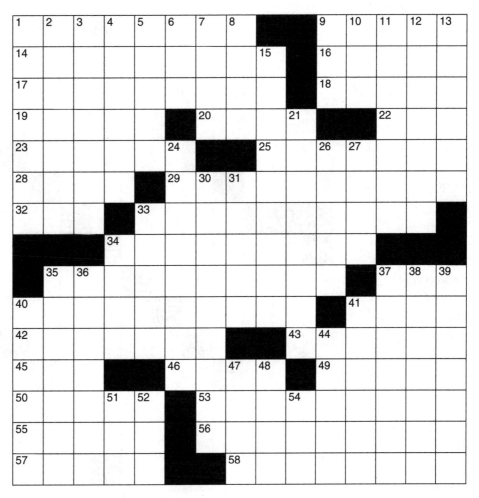

by Patrick Berry

ACROSS

1 Offer to host
8 W.W. II vessels
15 Expressed slight surprise
17 "But really . . ."
18 __ Empire
19 Deep-seated
20 What you might be overseas?
21 Part of A.M.A.: Abbr.
22 Principal
23 Leave in
24 Rx specification
25 Industry leader
26 Part of a place setting
27 Swelters
28 Absolutely correct
29 Relatives of spoonbills
31 Voyeur
32 Staggered
33 Many chains are found in them
34 Ticked off
35 Works at a museum, say
36 One of the girls
39 Going __
40 Gnats and mosquitoes
41 Powerful engine
42 Pipe holder?
43 Watch brand once worn by 007
44 One of 24
45 1959 #5 hit with the B-side "I've Cried Before"
48 What a board may be against
49 Euripides tragedy
50 Satyrs, say

DOWN

1 Mountains of __ (Genesis locale)
2 Strauss opera
3 "Trees" poet
4 Werner of "The Spy Who Came in From the Cold"
5 "In that __ . . ."
6 Hall-of-Fame outfielder Roush
7 Throws off
8 Flag carried on a knight's lance
9 Blake's "burning bright" cat
10 Pessimist
11 Outmoded: Abbr.
12 Three-time Haitian president
13 Super-wonderful
14 Make more attractive
16 Warriors with supposed powers of invisibility and shapeshifting
22 Ready for an on-air interview
23 "Your mama wears army boots" and such
25 Put a charge into?
26 Leans precariously
27 "L'Arlésienne" composer
28 Workout targets, informally
29 Copycat
30 Long-haired cat breed
31 Simple and serene
32 Fox relative
33 Old arm
35 Pale shades
36 Fought
37 Shot-putter, e.g.
38 Puts in
40 "Positive thinking" pioneer
41 Grounds for a medal
43 Pet
44 Place for a jerk?
46 "Captain Video" figures, for short
47 '50s politico

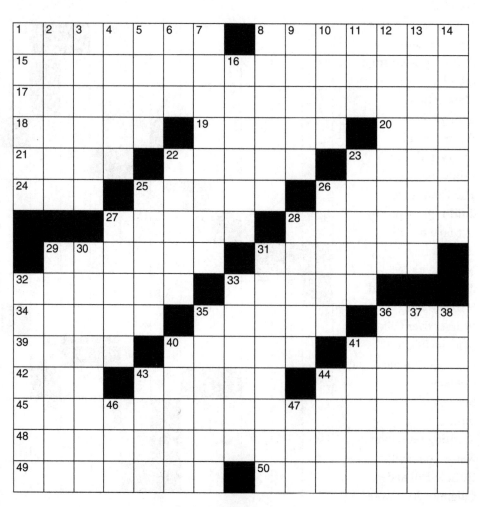

by Mangesh Ghogre and Doug Peterson

ACROSS

1 Begin
10 Donizetti heroine
15 Catches up to
16 Magnetron component
17 Relative of a spouse
19 "Just playin'"
20 Things often dropped in Harvard Yard?
21 Big name in winter vehicles
22 Fixer, perhaps
23 In the way of
24 Phony blazers
25 Birthplace of the Franciscan order
27 "Before My Birth" collagist, 1914
28 __-yo (cold treat, briefly)
29 With 36- and 39-Across, go from 1- to 61-Across
31 10-year-old Best Supporting Actress
33 Robert W. Service's "The Cremation of Sam __"
36 See 29-Across
37 Robert W. Service output
38 Soothing flora
39 See 29-Across
41 Bumped into
42 Bumped into
43 Razor target, maybe
47 Pack into a thick mass
50 Ottoman bigwig
51 Tan in a library
52 Anatomical ring
53 Direction de Paris à Nancy
54 Vegan gelatin substitute
55 Stopgap supervisor's duty
58 __ Montoya, swordsman in "The Princess Bride"
59 Prefixes featured on some maps
60 Baden-Powell of the Girl Guides
61 End

DOWN

1 One known for riding out of gear?
2 Brings out
3 Sends in
4 He'll "talk 'til his voice is hoarse"
5 The Who's "__ Hard"
6 __ Romanova, alter ego of Marvel's Black Widow
7 Landmark anime film of 1988
8 Many pulp heroes, in slang
9 Picking up skill?
10 Cheerful early risers
11 Preposition on a business-hours sign
12 Unit charge
13 "&" or "@," but not "and" or "at"
14 Restricted flight items
18 By yesterday, so to speak
23 Indication of some oxidation
24 Hug or kiss, maybe
26 Drink brand symbolized by a polar bear
27 39th vice president
30 "The Dark Knight Rises" director, 2012
31 Grammy category
32 What's typical
33 "Lordy!" in Lodi
34 Snow job?
35 Been chosen, as for office
40 One-two in the ring?
42 Pavlova portrayed one over 4,000 times
44 Storied place of worship
45 Eastern lodging
46 "2 Fast 2 Furious" co-star Gibson
48 Grand Caravan maker
49 Jumbles
50 One of Jacob's sons
53 Ser, across the Pyrenees
54 Loads
56 Piece of the street
57 __-fi

by Peter A. Collins

ACROSS

1 Hall-of-Fame rock band or its lead musician
8 It sends out lots of streams
15 Very long European link
16 Rust or combust
17 It flies on demand
18 Skunk, at times
19 Some P.D. personnel
20 One who may be on your case
22 The Spanish I love?
23 What a couple of people can play
25 Stand-out performances
26 Chocolate bar with a long biscuit and caramel
27 Subject of the 2003 book "Power Failure"
29 Without hesitation
30 Subsist on field rations?
31 Its flowers are very short-lived
33 Like a sawhorse's legs
35 Critical
36 Party staple
37 Catered to Windows shoppers?
41 Noodle taxers?
45 Observes
46 Abbr. after 8-Across
48 Last band in the Rock and Roll Hall of Fame, alphabetically
49 "The Hudsucker Proxy" director, 1994
50 Columbia and the like
52 French river or department
53 "__ mentioned . . ."
54 Images on some lab slides

56 Lima-to-Bogotá dir.
57 Frankenstein, e.g.
59 Its passengers were revolting
61 Theodore Roosevelt Island setting
62 Destroyer destroyer
63 Colorful cooler
64 Makeover options

DOWN

1 Like some milk
2 Sashimi staple
3 Changing place
4 Blockbuster?
5 Mediums for dummies, say: Abbr.
6 Where it all comes together?
7 Ex amount?

8 Appointment disappointments
9 Nationals, at one time
10 Flag
11 Tablet banner, say, briefly
12 Reserve
13 Inventory
14 Duped
21 Gradual, in some product names
24 Giant in fantasy
26 Bar that's set very high
28 Physicist Bohr
30 Display on a red carpet
32 Basic solution
34 Without hesitation, in brief
37 Does some outdoor pitching?

38 "Don't joke about that yet"
39 Took away bit by bit
40 Event occasioning 7-Down
41 Cryotherapy choice
42 Artificially small
43 What might take up residence?
44 Truncated trunks?
47 Zero times, in Zwickau
50 Back-pedaler's words
51 About 7% of it is American
54 Vapor: Prefix
55 Apple assistant
58 Lib. arts major
60 Coral __ (city near Oakland Pk., Fla.)

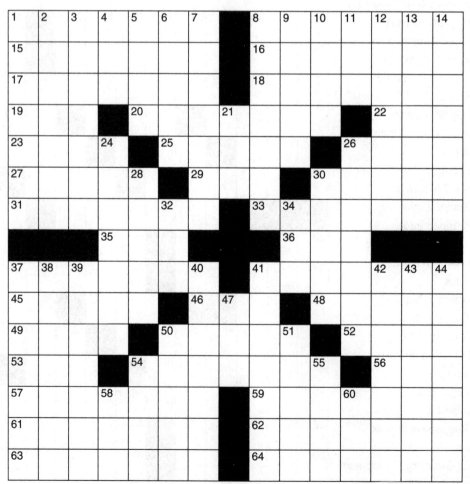

by Bruce R. Sutphin

ACROSS

1 Forest newcomer
5 Group whose last Top 40 hit was "When All Is Said and Done"
9 To-do list
14 Sound after call waiting?
15 Sense, as a 14-Across
16 Nobel winner Joliot-Curie
17 Turkey sticker
20 "Everybody Is __" (1970 hit)
21 Response to a threat
22 Old co. with overlapping globes in its logo
23 1960s civil rights leader __ Brown
25 Katey who portrayed TV's Peg Bundy
27 Benchwarmer's plea
33 Drain
34 Bobby's follower?
35 Fibonacci, notably
36 Hockey Hall of Fame nickname
38 Alternative to ZzzQuil
40 Stat. for Re, La or Ti
41 "__ needed"
43 Papa __ (Northeast pizza chain)
45 Now in
46 "That subject's off the table!"
49 Luster
50 They have edible shells
51 Whse. sight
53 "Philosophy will clip an angel's wings" writer
56 French class setting
59 Universal query?
62 Uncle Sam, say
63 One featuring a Maltese cross
64 Turkic word for "island"
65 Browser history list
66 Couldn't discard in crazy eights, say
67 Court suspensions

DOWN

1 Relief provider, for short
2 Blasts through
3 "And now?"
4 Sealing worker
5 "Per-r-rfect!"
6 __-red
7 Alfred H. __ Jr., founding director of MoMA
8 Like G.I.'s, per recruiting ads
9 Interval
10 Were present?
11 Gets payback
12 Sensed
13 They may be used in veins
18 They may be used around veins
19 All-Star Infante
24 Drone
26 1998 hit from the album "Surfacing"
27 False start?
28 Stockholder?
29 Like some hemoglobin
30 __-A
31 Plantation habitation
32 Cybermemo
37 Something taken on the stand
39 Ring
42 They're on hunts
44 Revolving feature
47 Revolving features?
48 "Psst . . . buddy"
51 1/20 tons: Abbr.
52 Whence the word "bong"
54 Day of the week of Jul. 4, 1776
55 Wizened up
57 Indiana, e.g., to Lafayette
58 Some use electric organs
60 River Shannon's Lough __
61 Sudoku segment

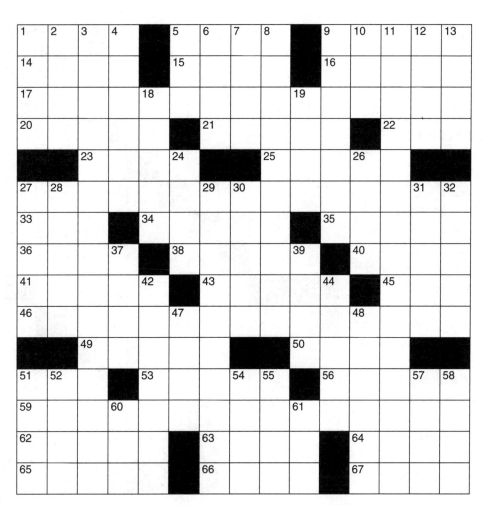

by Peter A. Collins

46

ACROSS

1 1999 rap hit featuring Snoop Dogg
9 "Sin City" actress
13 Classic TV family
15 Represent
16 45°, for 1
18 Wild things?
19 Puts on eBay again
20 Cuban province where Castro was born
22 Zoological groups
23 Diamond deal
24 Software plug-in
25 Mode of transportation in a 1969 #1 hit
26 Filmdom family name
27 Israel's Sea of __
28 Silence fillers
29 Informal name of the 45th state
30 Softball question
33 Clean, now
34 Songbird Mitchell
35 Turkey __, baseball Hall-of-Famer from the Negro leagues
37 Breaks
38 They get tested
39 __ system, part of the brain that regulates emotion, behavior and long-term memory
40 2000s CBS sitcom
41 Sextet at Woodstock
42 "El Condor __" (1970 Simon & Garfunkel hit)
43 Golda Meir and Yitzhak Rabin led it
45 Division d'une carte
46 Place of outdoor meditation
47 Mock words of understanding
48 Price of an opera?

DOWN

1 Gangster nickname
2 "Carmen" figure
3 Covers
4 Share a secret with
5 From the Forbidden City
6 Bad impressions?
7 Poverty, metaphorically
8 Dutch city ESE of Amsterdam
9 Shape shifters?
10 Try to hear better, maybe
11 Knock-down-drag-out
12 First name in shooting
14 Winter set
17 Didn't make it home, say
21 Arm
23 Email ancestors
25 "Wordplay" vocalist, 2005
27 "In your dreams!"
29 Mary __ (doomed ship)
30 Italian region that's home to Milan
31 Chances that a year ends with any particular digit
32 Florida's Key __
33 Musician who arranged the theme from "2001"
34 Fruit-filled pastry
35 Where to bury the hatchet?
36 Olympic ice dancing gold medalist Virtue and others
37 __ Alley
38 Hypercompetitive
39 About 40–60 beats per minute
41 Volume measure
44 Volume measure

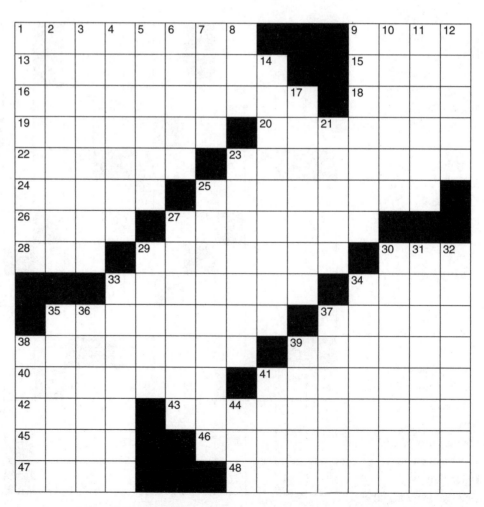

by David Steinberg

ACROSS

1 Wiped the floor with
16 Use of blockades, say
17 Western daily
18 Lobby
19 Watch things
20 Limited edition?
21 Suffix with electr-
22 Blasting, musically
24 Bay, say . . . or bring to bay
28 Tempest, to Theodor
31 Bellyaches
33 __ Rose
34 One may be tapped out
37 Brunch orders, briefly
38 McKinley's Ohio birthplace
39 Title priestess of opera
40 Aim
42 Setting of 10, maybe
43 Sony output
44 Bulldogs' sch.
46 Painter __ della Francesca
48 Certain advertising medium
55 It's not word-for-word
56 Old French epics
57 Idolizes

DOWN

1 1970s–'80s sitcom setting
2 "I'm __" (Friday declaration)
3 Doctor's orders
4 Passing people
5 What Hamilton called the wealthy
6 "Sure, let's try"
7 __ Arden Oplev, director of "The Girl With the Dragon Tattoo"
8 Mid third-century year
9 Gershwin biographer David
10 Guarders with droopy ears and pendulous lips
11 Some collectible lithographs
12 It hasn't happened before
13 Sans spice
14 Sought-after rock group?
15 Fun or laugh follower
22 Send quickly, in a way
23 Finders' keepers?
25 What stars may indicate
26 Cause of a class struggle?
27 Allure alternative
28 Sun blocker
29 Pearl Harbor attack initiator
30 Polaris bear
31 Limb-entangling weapon
32 Second-greatest period in the history of something
35 1931 Best Picture
36 Utility bill details
41 Light measures
43 Like much arable land
45 "I __ Lonely" (1954 hit for the Four Knights)
46 Lead-in to deux or trois
47 Particular paean penner
48 Ozone destroyers, for short
49 "What's Hecuba to him, __ to Hecuba": Hamlet
50 Sinatra's "Meet __ the Copa"
51 Biblical miracle setting
52 Police dept. personage
53 Touch
54 Law school newbie

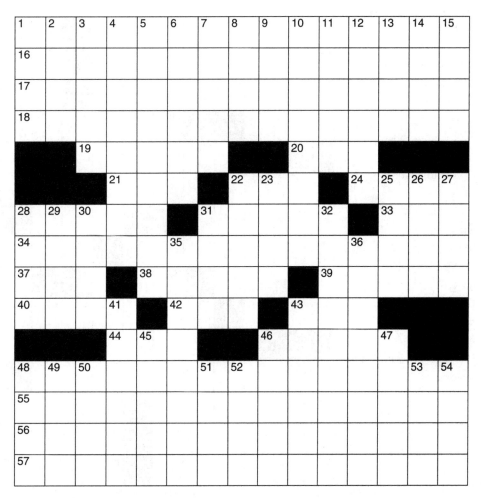

by Martin Ashwood-Smith

48

ACROSS

1 Common catch off the coast of Maryland
9 Light, in a way
15 Crude alternative
16 Jewelry box item
17 Like a bout on an undercard
18 Dickens's Miss Havisham, famously
19 ID clincher
20 Challenge to ambulance chasers
22 Arcade game prize grabber
24 Fiacre, to taxi drivers
27 "__ reminder . . ."
30 Nook occupier
31 Toshiba competitor
32 Some camcorders
33 Besmirch
36 Isaac Bashevis Singer settings
38 Culmination
39 Only proper noun in the Beatles' "Revolution"
41 "Something to Talk About" singer, 1991
42 Golf commentator's subject
43 Classic kitschy wall hanging
46 Slip for a skirt?
47 "Billy Bathgate" novelist
50 Ex-G.I.'s org.
53 Washington State mascot
54 Pre-W.W. I in automotive history
57 "If music be the food of love . . ." speaker in "Twelfth Night"
58 Cry of despair
59 Nothing: It.
60 Periods of warming . . . or cooling off

DOWN

1 M asset
2 Royal Arms of England symbol
3 Bone under a watchband
4 The Orange Bowl is played on it: Abbr.
5 Acupuncturist's concern
6 Croupier's stick material
7 Acknowledges
8 Tab carrier in a bar?
9 Tourist attraction on Texas's Pedernales River
10 Face in a particular direction
11 "Champagne for One" sleuth
12 Shot, informally
13 Serena Williams, often
14 Novel in Joyce Carol Oates's Wonderland Quartet
21 Exasperates
22 Cauldron stirrer
23 "The Avengers" villain, 2012
24 Bit of sachet stuffing
25 Classroom clickers of old
26 Singer who once sang a song to Kramer on "Seinfeld"
27 When "Ave Maria" is sung in "Otello"
28 1970s pact partly negotiated in Helsinki
29 Right hands: Abbr.
32 Arena
34 Orange garnish for a sushi roll
35 Fox hunt cry
37 Bay, for one
40 Prompt a buzzer on "The Price Is Right"
43 Unoccupied
44 Massive, in Metz
45 Block
46 Keep from taking off, as a plane with low visibility
47 Nobel category: Abbr.
48 Loughlin or Petty of Hollywood
49 Italian actress Eleonora
50 Let it all out
51 Unoccupied
52 Rolls of dough
55 One of the Ms. Pac-Man ghosts
56 "There is no __ except stupidity": Wilde

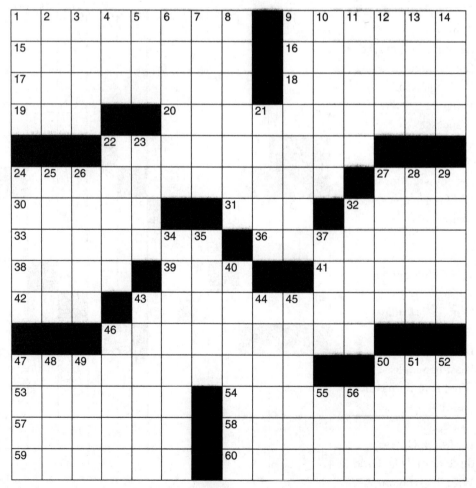

by Brad Wilber

ACROSS

1 African city of 4+ million whose name means, literally, "haven of peace"
12 Seeing things
14 "Why such a fuss?"
16 Start of a Jewish holiday?
17 Put one's two cents in?
18 Arizona's Agua ___ River
19 Not natural for
21 Like Beethoven's Piano Sonata No. 6 or 22
24 Tilting figure: Abbr.
25 ___ Ximénez (dessert sherry)
26 Manipulative health care worker
29 Smash letters
30 Destroy, informally
32 Range ridges
33 Classified
35 Eatery where the Tony Award was born
38 Pitch
39 Juan's "Hey!"
42 Perseveres
44 Some Deco pieces
46 Lead film festival characters?
47 Rhineland Campaign's arena: Abbr.
48 Frito-Lay snack
50 Silver of fivethirtyeight.com
52 California city near Fullerton
54 Author Janowitz
55 Opening line of a 1966 #1 Beatles hit
59 One-hit wonder
60 Events for some antiquers

DOWN

1 Demonstration exhortation
2 A bee might light on it
3 Some N.F.L.'ers
4 Irritate
5 Dopes
6 Restoration notation
7 Even though
8 Polynesian island chain?
9 Lee with an Oscar
10 Home row sequence
11 Kalahari Desert dweller
12 Irritability
13 Femme canonisée
14 Deli menu subheading
15 Foundation for some roofing
20 Silence
22 Verges on
23 Anticipate
27 Mind
28 Irritable state
31 Election surprise
33 What some bombs result in, in brief
34 Fanciful notions
35 Dead
36 Pair of boxers?
37 Give a makeover
39 Pontiac and others
40 "Star Trek" extra
41 It's definitely not the short answer
43 "That's that"
45 Fix a key problem?
49 Kind of yoga
51 Important info for people with connections
53 Clément with two Oscar-winning films
56 Düsseldorf direction
57 La la lead-in
58 Allen of play-by-play

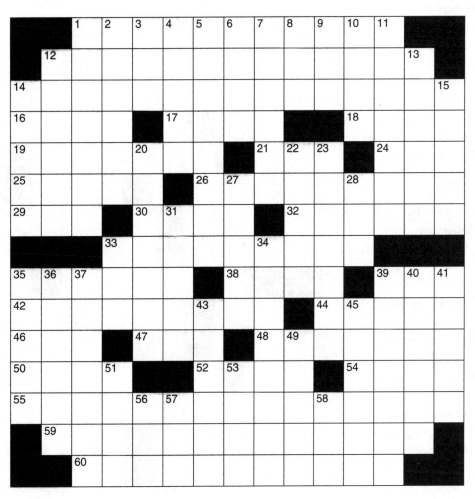

by Alan Arbesfeld

ACROSS

1 Their drinks are not on the house
9 Rough limestone regions with sinkholes and caverns
15 Novel title character with a "brief, wondrous life"
16 Hawaii's Forbidden Isle
17 ". . . period!"
19 One buzzing off?
20 Three Stooges display
21 Some lab leaders, for short
22 Like most hall-of-fame inductees: Abbr.
23 Gave belts or socks
24 Swamp
25 Female friends, to Francisco
27 Early-millennium year
28 Jet black
29 Some are soft-shell
30 Spread out
32 He cast the Killing Curse on Dumbledore
33 What the Flying Wallendas refuse to use
34 Powerful Hindu deities
38 That same number of
40 Diner's words of thanks
41 Unlucky accidents, old-style
44 Co. led by Baryshnikov in the 1980s
45 It broke up in the age of dinosaurs
46 Not procrastinating
47 Midday assignation, in slang
49 Stink
50 Olive ___
51 More pointed

52 Give an underhanded hand?
53 Assertion more likely to be correct if 8-Down is given
56 Decision makers
57 Axis, e.g.
58 "Fingers crossed"
59 Whose eyes Puck squeezes magical juice on

DOWN

1 "Well done!"
2 With no dissenters
3 Common result of a slipped disk
4 Foil feature
5 Realty ad abbr.
6 Lies ahead

7 What a vacay provides
8 What an interrogator might administer
9 Bring home, as a run
10 Light as a feather
11 One in a cage
12 Confined
13 Vast historical region controlled by the Mongols
14 Kingdom next to Kent
18 See 24-Down
23 They aid responses, in brief
24 With 18-Down, life today
26 Transcend
30 Speaking of repeatedly, to a Brit
31 1984 award for Elmore Leonard

35 Drifting type
36 Good hand holding in Omaha Hi-Lo
37 It has the densest fur of any animal
39 Alpine skier Julia who won Olympic gold in 2006
41 Still-produced stuff
42 Slangy segue
43 Awful accident
45 Hazards
48 Afresh
51 Film and theater
52 Actor Rickman who played 32-Across
54 Low numero
55 ___ Fáil (Irish coronation stone)

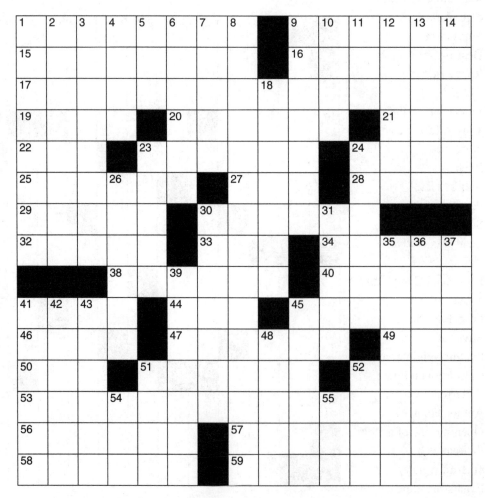

by David Woolf

1

2

3

4

5

6

7

```
H O N O R S . O R S . E D A M
A M A Z O N . B A T F L I P S
L A D Y D I . I M A L L S E T
T H E M S T H E B R E A K S .
S A R A . I S L E S .
. N E E D . E D H E L M S
H E A D T R I P . M O R E
A C C I D E N T S H A P P E N
N C A A . A C I D T E S T
S E I S M I C . E T S Y .
. U T A H N . S A S S
J U S T A S I T H O U G H T
Z E P P E L I N . E M I G R E
E N C O D I N G . E N T R E E
E A S T . A G E . D I S O W N
```

8

```
P A N E L . M I M I . A P B S
A S I D E . E V E R . L S A T
T A K E A B R E A K . L O N E
S H O R T L I S T . F O R K .
Y I N . H O T . A R T I S T
. C E O . A C N E . A H A
. W O R D P R O C E S S O R
. P I N S T R I P E S U I T
F A K E E Y E L A S H E S .
C P I . A P P S . T I S .
C A P O T E . C O P . A K A
. B E D S . S T A R P O W E R
R E D O . R I S K S I T A L L
P A I R . B R A E . N O I S E
I R A S . G I R D . G E T O N
```

9

```
N A Z A R E N E . R A J A H S
O R A L E X A M . A M U L E T
D O M I N A T E . D E S A D E
R U B . E L T R A I N . T B A
A S E A . T E S L A . D E E M
M E Z Z O . R O O T B E E R S
A S I A N . S N E E R I N G .
. L E I . S I T .
. D E E P S I G H . S I L E X
K A L A M A Z O O . K E A N E
A Y E S . B O O T Y . S T A R
P T A . M E D D L E S . E M O
L I N T E L . J A S O N F O X
A M O R A L . O V E R H E R E
N E R U D A . B A S E L E S S
```

10

```
E M M A . D E S C . S F P D
B A R T R I V I A . O O H E D
B I T T E R E N D . P R I M O
. S E N S E S . A L O T
S P I N A R T . T A N L I N E
P E N A L . H O S T E L S .
L E A V E N E D . F A I T H S
A L T E . A N D S O . C I A O
T E T L E Y . E A R C A N D Y
. E G O S U R F . A R E N A
B A N A N A S . E R N E S T S
L U T Z . Y E O M A N .
A R I E L . D R O V E N U T S
H A V R E . T I D E S O V E R
. L E S T . O N E S . T A X I
```

11

```
L E T S D A N C E . S T U B S
I M O N A R O L L . T U P A C
N O W O R R I E S . A S T I R
E T A . N O R A . N I K O L A
A I W A . W O N T O N . Y O W
R O A S T . N E R F . S O U L
A N Y W A Y . D E E P C U T S
. E M A J . Y E A H .
W H O L E H O G . S I N G E S
H A L L . W H O A . N O O N E
A V E . D E N O V O . Z E T A
T E M P E H . D E B T . S E W
A N I O N . H E R E W E A R E
M O S E S . E A S Y A S P I E
I T S M E . P R E S S S E N D
```

12

```
. A Y C A R A M B A . M I L D
T R O U B A D O U R . O B I E
G E O D E S I S T S . B A N C
I N H D . A S T O R . N G O
F O O L E D . S N A C K E D
. T O E T A G S . W H E R E
. B A R R A G E . A R I D
T R U S T E X E R C I S E .
G R I D . S W O R N I N .
A A N D P . N E S T L E S
B I G Y U K S . T I E R E D
B L T . G N A R S . T H R U
A M O R . O C E A N S T A T E
N I N E . T H E G E N E R A L
A X E D . S A F E W O R D S .
```

13

```
A M O N G . I G A . A S A P
P O K E R . F O O L . D U L L
S T O N E H E N G E . B R I O
E E K A M O U S E . B L E E P
. . . L S D . T H R O W N .
C A R R I E S A T O R C H .
A R I A N A . L E G . K Y L O
L E N D S . H E R . T E N A M
M A G I . M I X . C O R O N A
. B A N A N A S F O S T E R
. S E L E C T . I L L .
S T A T E . H U L A S K I R T
N O R I . B I L L T H E C A T
O V E R . A N T S . E N E M Y
W E R E . M T A . D O R A L
```

14

```
C A T T L E T H I E F . I S M
A G O R A P H O B I A . G O O
M I N I S T E R I N G . O R E
P L O P S . C A S S E T T E S
Y E W S . M O T E . N E A L
. V A N I S H . A N O N
F A N D A N G O . E L P A S O
E Q U A L T O . G R O O M E D
S U M M E R . P L O T T E R S
T A B S . A L I E N S .
. V E E S . A N N S . M U S S
A I R L I F T E D . S A N T A
A T T . G R E T A G E R W I G
R A E . N A T A L I E C O L E
P E N . S T O R E F R O N T S
```

15

```
D A M P . S N U B S . A T R A
O B O E . T E N E T . B R A N
W O O T . E X T R A P O I N T
D O N T G E T A N Y I D E A S
. Q U O R U M . Z E S T Y
S P U R T . P E R E Z .
H E A T H . D E R A I L E D
O A K L A N D . I N O N E G O
P R E E M I E S . V A M O S
. C L O T H . E M O T E
A S A M I . J O I N I N .
S C R A T C H A N D S N I F F
P O T T Y H U M O R . U C L A
E R I E . U T E R I . T E A K
N E E D . M U S E S . E S T E
```

16

```
V I B E . S A B A N . A B E T
O P E N S E S A M E . S E G O
C A T C H A S C A T C H C A N
E D T . A L E K . S A L A D S
. E N D . T S P . T A U .
C O R E R . S E A H O R S E S
O S G O O D . A T E . E X E
S C E N E O F T H E C R I M E
T A T . H A D . L O O T E D
A R M C H A I R S . N A S T Y
. O R A . L I T . D D T .
L O V A T O . V A S E . H E Y
S H I V E R M E T I M B E R S
A N N E . S C R U B N U R S E
T O G S . O A S E S . B E E R
```

17

```
R A B B I . C L A P S . J O G
I M O L D . Z O R R O . U R L
P E N A L . A B B E Y . I D A
O N E B E D R O O M . A C E S
F R I S C O . R E N D E R S
F A N . H U L A . D O O B I E
. G A L O S H . T R A N S
. G R E T A T H U N B E R G .
F A I N T . R E L O A D
I M F R E E . S K I D . P G A
R E F E R E E . S A L O O N
E T E S . L E A S E T O O W N
L I D . O P R A H . A U D I O
I M O . N O I R E . L I L L Y
T E N . S T E P S . L E E D S
```

18

```
S A T E L L I T E S T A T E S
A D E L A I D E S L A M E N T
M A R I N E I N S U R A N C E
S I N G I N G T O G E T H E R
. R E I . S I E . I D I O .
. S B A . T R O T . S U M O
. L I S . R O Z . R A H
S N E E R A T . G U E S S S O
H E X . E M I . T A C .
A Z O V . M A P A . L A S .
. R I M Y . A R M . R T S
S A C R I F I C I A L L A M B
A M I G L A D T O S E E Y O U
G A S O L I N E S T A T I O N
A N T S I N O N E S P A N T S
```

19

```
M O V E B A C K ■ B B K I N G
I R E A L I Z E ■ L I E S O N
D E L T A R A Y ■ U G A N D A
■ V A D E R ■ P E G ■ ■ T E T
S P E W E D ■ R A J A H ■ ■ ■
I O T A S ■ F A C E M A S K S
G O R Y ■ K A F K A E S Q U E
H B O ■ K I T T E N S ■ U R L
T A P D A N C E R S ■ N A T E
S H E D T E A R S ■ D O R I C
■ T E S T S ■ ■ D I V E S T ■
A N N ■ M C S ■ C U R E D ■ ■
T O O T O O ■ P O P E L E O X
T H E A S P ■ I D E C L A R E
N O L O S E ■ T E D T A L K S
```

20

```
F O S H I Z Z L E ■ C A N S T
A T H E N A E U M ■ E P O C H
S T A N D I N G O ■ L I T H E
T O R ■ O R I G ■ G L A M O R
O M I T ■ E T A L I I ■ U L E
N A N A S ■ H G T V ■ S C A T
E N G I N E ■ E Y E ■ T H R O
■ I N L A W ■ R U N A T ■ ■ ■
M A S T ■ T A B ■ P A Y O L A
A R C S ■ S N U B ■ P A L I N
N E A ■ P A S C A L ■ T O O T
M A R M O T ■ O M A R ■ O N O
A R I A L ■ A L A N A R K I N
D U N N O ■ L I K E C R A Z Y
E G G O S ■ E C O S Y S T E M
```

21

```
C H I L L A X ■ G A G A R I N
H A V E A G O ■ A D R I A N A
U V I N D E X ■ T E R R I F Y
M R E D ■ S O P H S ■ E S O S
P E D A L ■ X K E ■ I D E M ■
■ H O L O G R A M ■ H A D ■ ■
D E J A V U ■ S E X S C E N E
E X E N E M Y ■ R I T A L I N
B A L D S P O T ■ O U T L A Y
S M L ■ E S U R A N C E ■ ■ ■
■ P O E T ■ L I D ■ K R A U T
F A S T ■ G L O A T ■ W N B A
I P H O N E S ■ P A R A D O X
L E O N I N E ■ T R O U B L E
A R T S A L E ■ S T Y L E T S
```

22

```
Y I D D I S H ■ A I R M A I L
A R I A N N A ■ C L E A N S E
W I S H F U L D R I N K I N G
E N B L O C ■ E Y E T E S T S
D A E ■ ■ K F C ■ D A G ■ ■ ■
■ L A E ■ A A H ■ ■ O S H A ■
T W I T T E R F O L L O W E R
O N E T O G O ■ P A Y D I R T
S E V E N O F D I A M O N D S
S T E N ■ F E N ■ E N G ■ ■ ■
■ D E T ■ A G O ■ ■ F U R ■ ■
T R I A X I A L ■ W I N O N A
M I D N I G H T I N P A R I S
E L E C T R A ■ D E S P I T E
N E M E S E S ■ O R E S T E S
```

23

```
R E S T A I N ■ ■ C O M E T S
O S C A R N O D S ■ O P A Q U E
S T O R Y B O O K ■ B A K U L A
Y O W Z A ■ K N O W ■ L E A S T
■ A N S ■ T R I B ■ A L A S ■
■ V O N ■ M S T ■ N A T S ■ ■
L I T T L E L E A G U E T E A M
I S T H A T A L L T H E R E I S
B A S E B A L L D I A M O N D S
■ A S N O ■ A P U ■ N Y E ■ ■
W A S P ■ A M F M ■ S K G ■ ■
A S H E S ■ S O A K ■ A C O A T
I S O M E R ■ A T A G L A N C E
T E J A N O ■ M O V I E S E T S
S T I N G Y ■ A L L E G E S
```

24

```
C R A Z I E R ■ A B B O T S
A U G U S T U S ■ B A L B O A
C S I M I A M I ■ C M A J O R
A T L A S ■ B L T S ■ M E L C
O Y E ■ L A I R ■ M E C C A
■ M A E ■ C U T E ■ T A S
■ P O S T M O D E R N I S M
■ D R S T R A N G E L O V E
D E A T H I N V E N I C E
O M G ■ M P A A ■ I N K
M O M M A ■ G L E E ■ S A C
I T A S ■ F E L L ■ S M I T E
N A T T E R ■ E I T H E R O R
O P I A T E ■ Y O U O W E M E
S E C R E T ■ T O P L E S S
```

25

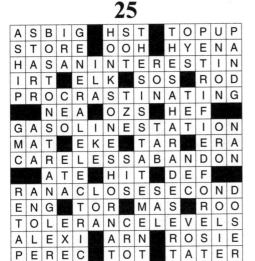

```
A S B I G ■ H S T ■ T O P U P
S T O R E ■ ■ O O H ■ H Y E N A
H A S A N I N T E R E S T I N
I R T ■ E L K ■ S O S ■ R O D
P R O C R A S T I N A T I N G
■ N E A ■ O Z S ■ H E F ■
G A S O L I N E S T A T I O N
M A T ■ E K E ■ T A R ■ E R A
C A R E L E S S A B A N D O N
■ A T E ■ H I T ■ D E F ■
R A N A C L O S E S E C O N D
E N G ■ T O R ■ M A S ■ R O O
T O L E R A N C E L E V E L S
A L E X I ■ A R N ■ R O S I E
P E R E C ■ T O T ■ T A T E R
```

26

```
A M I W R O N G ■ J U L I E
G A M E O V E R ■ S O N A T A
E X H I B I T A ■ O N A P A R
N O U S ■ D I V I N G B E L L
D U R S T ■ Z I T I ■ A L I G
A T T ■ A C E T E N ■ S P A R
■ E P O N Y M ■ T H I N E
A M E X E S ■ T E E N S Y
D A V I D ■ M E O W E D ■
A R E S ■ C A N N O N ■ M A T
P I N T ■ O N I T ■ S L U S H
T A K E F L I G H T ■ A R C O
S C E N E I ■ M E R R Y M E N
T H E C A N ■ A Q U A L U N G
O I L E R ■ S T E W A R D S
```

27

```
C A T S P A W ■ E M A I L E D
O N A T E A R ■ M I S S I V E
M A K E T H E B E S T O F I T
E G E R ■ S N A R E R ■ E N O
D R A N K ■ L Y R A ■ I C U
U A L ■ O P E L ■ L A S E R
E M O ■ B E T T Y S ■ I V S
■ O V E R T H E E D G E ■
■ T K O ■ T E E T E R ■ R C T
B R A N S ■ J I M I ■ Y A O
U A R ■ U S N A ■ B A S R A
M I O ■ I C I C L E ■ R H O S
P L U M T U C K E R E D O U T
P E N R O S E ■ D I V E R S E
O R D E R I N ■ S C E N T E D
```

28

```
Y A W N ■ S T A B ■ L I E S
E C H O ■ T O U R ■ L A D L E
C H A R L E S D E G A U L L E
C O M M E R C I A L B R E A K
H O S A N N A ■ C O O E D ■
■ R I O ■ P H A R L A P ■
D I V A N ■ W A I T S ■ W E B
E P E E ■ C H I N S ■ C A N E
W A N ■ S L A N G ■ D A Y N E
■ D E S P I T E ■ G E L ■
■ Z A L E S ■ P A N A C E A
Y O U C A N T W I N E M A L L
E V E R Y T H I N G B A G E L
G A L E S ■ A N T E ■ R E N O
G L A D ■ T E A S ■ I S A Y
```

29

```
T A B L E C L O T H ■ S E G A
M I R A C L E G R O ■ M A R S
A M Y P O E H L E R ■ A R E S
N E N ■ A M E N R A ■ L G A
■ E S T A ■ D O N ■ M A I
P O S T M E N ■ I R T ■ O R L
O P E N E D ■ I N S I G N I A
R E N A L ■ R O G ■ B O R O N
T R E S T L E S ■ B O W O U T
L A G ■ R E A ■ O L D N E S S
A T A ■ O E D ■ P A Y S ■
N I L ■ E R O T I C ■ P H D
D O E S ■ S N E A K A P E E K
I N S P ■ A L L T E R R A I N
A S E A ■ T Y L E R P E R R Y
```

30

```
S N A I L S H E L L ■ A P E D
H A R R Y C A R A Y ■ X O X O
E S C A L A T O R S ■ E L I A
A S H I E R ■ Y E S L E T S
T A I L S ■ Q A N D A ■ A L I
H U E S ■ S T Y X ■ X A X I S
■ S P I N ■ L O R E N A
B O X S T E P ■ W I N F R E Y
U S E T A X ■ Z A N Y ■
M O R A N ■ T E N T ■ R E B A
P L O ■ C L U E D ■ B E T E L
S E X S H O P ■ S A S H A Y
O M I T ■ W E B B A N N E R S
F I N D ■ P L A I N J A N E S
F O G S ■ H O R S E O P E R A
```

31

```
WASATCH ▌ KIDNAPS
ARTSALE ▌ SHOOFLY
SOAPBOX ▌ TRISTAN
AMI ▌ ODAMAE ▌ TESS
BANCO ▌ GAR ▌ TERM ▌
ISSO ▌ DRT ▌ YAPSAT
▌ THEATEAM ▌ ITO
JULYIVMDCCLXXVI
ABO ▌ HASACHAT ▌▌
MESIAL ▌ MET ▌ ROMA
▌ RENT ▌ JON ▌ SATAN
AGFA ▌ SUNTAN ▌ TUG
BEARCAT ▌ RCADOME
RECURVE ▌ INITIAL
IKETTES ▌ CELSIUS
```

32

```
JUSTADROP ▌ STARK
ANTONIONI ▌ REGAL
CRANKCASE ▌ SMOTE
KEY ▌ HONEST ▌ PURE
PASS ▌ TSR ▌ RATTAN
ODIOUS ▌ VEIL ▌ ICE
TYNAN ▌ GENTLESEX
▌ RUSE ▌ DEBS ▌
SWISSALPS ▌ UNDER
HAS ▌ ELSE ▌ ETERNE
OREIDA ▌ RNA ▌ SICS
OWED ▌ DESOTO ▌ VAT
TOYED ▌ MODELLERS
AROSE ▌ INORDERTO
TNUTS ▌ LAZYSUSAN
```

33

```
ASSET ▌ TESTMATCH
STALE ▌ APPIANWAY
QANDA ▌ RAINSTORM
UNDER ▌ HUTCHISON
IDBRACELET ▌ LOLA
TEA ▌ TREES ▌ CAMEL
HERB ▌ ALT ▌ SOBERS
▌ EATS ▌ SHOO ▌
ACHEBE ▌ SEE ▌ ROSE
BRATS ▌ BITES ▌ WPA
RUSH ▌ LANATURNER
EMBOWERED ▌ REGAL
ABEVIGODA ▌ EVOKE
SLEEPONIT ▌ LUAUS
TENNESSEE ▌ YELPS
```

34

```
THEWHO ▌ SNAP ▌ JET
RENAIL ▌ TOBESURE
ANGLED ▌ AMBROSIA
YIELDS ▌ SEAOTTER
SELA ▌ ASH ▌ ETHIC ▌
▌ COWHERB ▌ AFAR
ALTER ▌ OSHA ▌ TINO
LOESSER ▌ INAHEAP
ASST ▌ VTEN ▌ LADLE
SATE ▌ EUROPOP ▌
▌ LAVIN ▌ OSH ▌ POGS
PATENTED ▌ ONESET
IMONFIRE ▌ BANKSY
NORSEMAN ▌ IDEATE
ESS ▌ REST ▌ CADRES
```

35

```
KIDNEYBEAN ▌ LATE
ANYONEELSE ▌ ERIS
TRENCHCOAT ▌ GENT
ZED ▌ AIRFRANCE
▌ LULU ▌ ULULATE
SHIITES ▌ LIST ▌
WARGAME ▌ EXTENDS
UHOH ▌ NCAA
MANTRAS ▌ BRADAWL
▌ SUVA ▌ REVERSE
SEVENAM ▌ UBER ▌
PLECTRUMS ▌ GWB
LEGO ▌ IRAQIDINAR
IVAN ▌ CAYUGALAKE
TEND ▌ EISENHOWER
```

36

```
OMAHA ▌ ELMS ▌ SERF
HELEN ▌ KICKBOXER
CAPRI ▌ GERALDINE
ATHOME ▌ SITUATED
LEANERS ▌ BEEP ▌
CABS ▌ REF ▌ BOOST
UTE ▌ NAILCLIPPER
TET ▌ ANNULAR ▌ ELI
TRIBUTEBAND ▌ NFC
ASCOT ▌ SIC ▌ PESO
▌ AIRS ▌ REORDER
SCOTLAND ▌ THEFED
ARTMUSEUM ▌ ALIKE
KATESPADE ▌ RARER
EBON ▌ SKEW ▌ EWERS
```

37

A	T	W	A	R	■	F	L	E	E	■	S	A	P	S
B	U	R	M	A	■	R	A	I	L	■	C	L	A	W
O	N	I	O	N	R	I	N	G	S	■	R	E	N	E
D	E	S	K	■	O	N	T	H	E	L	E	V	E	L
E	S	T	■	P	U	G	E	T	■	E	W	E	L	L
■	B	A	L	L	E	R	I	N	A	S	■			
P	R	A	G	U	E	■	N	E	E	D	■	P	B	S
D	Y	N	A	S	T	S	■	S	A	F	A	R	I	S
Q	E	D	■	S	T	E	P	■	R	O	D	E	O	S
■	P	I	E	A	L	A	M	O	D	E	■			
G	E	O	R	G	■	T	A	C	I	T	■	M	A	P
E	R	G	O	N	O	M	I	C	S	■	L	P	G	A
I	R	I	S	■	B	A	T	E	S	M	O	T	E	L
C	O	V	E	■	I	T	E	S	■	I	R	E	N	E
O	R	E	S	■	T	E	D	S	■	L	E	D	T	O

38

P	E	D	I	C	A	B	■	B	R	A	P	A	D	S
A	R	I	G	A	T	O	■	E	A	T	E	N	U	P
P	A	N	A	R	A	B	■	R	I	H	A	N	N	A
A	S	K	■	L	L	B	■	T	S	A	R	I	S	M
■	T	O	O	L	S	■	I	N	L	E	T	S	■	
J	U	S	T	A	S	E	C	O	N	D				
U	N	I	O	N	S	H	O	P	S	■	M	O	E	T
B	U	R	P	S	■	E	N	E	■	W	E	L	S	H
A	M	I	S	■	M	A	C	N	C	H	E	E	S	E
■	R	I	D	E	S	H	O	T	G	U	N			
S	T	R	A	W	S	■	S	E	A	L	S	■		
W	E	E	L	A	S	S	■	C	L	E	■	I	R	E
A	P	L	E	N	T	Y	■	R	U	B	S	O	U	T
B	E	A	R	D	E	N	■	E	P	I	C	W	I	N
S	E	X	T	A	P	E	■	T	A	T	I	A	N	A

39

M	I	C	H	E	L	E	B	A	C	H	M	A	N	N
S	T	R	A	T	E	G	I	C	R	O	U	T	E	S
T	H	E	L	A	T	E	L	A	T	E	S	H	O	W
■	A	T	T	S	■	R	I	P	■	S	E	E	N	■
N	C	I	S	■	S	I	O	U	X	■	D	I	A	Z
C	A	N	■	E	P	A	U	L	E	T	■	S	T	E
O	N	S	T	A	R	■	S	C	R	A	M	M	E	D
■	A	S	I	F	■	O	O	P	S	■				
A	F	L	U	T	T	E	R	■	X	E	S	O	U	T
D	O	E	■	S	E	R	A	P	E	S	■	V	S	O
O	R	A	L	■	S	R	T	A	S	■	B	E	B	E
■	S	V	E	N	■	A	R	I	■	T	E	R	P	■
H	U	E	V	O	S	R	A	N	C	H	E	R	O	S
U	R	B	A	N	D	I	C	T	I	O	N	A	R	Y
P	E	E	R	A	S	S	E	S	S	M	E	N	T	S

40

P	O	V	E	R	T	Y	R	O	W	■	G	A	R	R
U	R	A	N	I	U	M	O	R	E	■	E	P	E	E
C	A	R	R	O	T	C	A	K	E	■	L	P	G	A
E	N	Y	A	■	U	A	R	■	D	I	A	L	U	P
■	G	A	S	■	P	E	N	T	E	L	■			
E	S	T	E	R	■	S	T	E	A	D	I	C	A	M
W	A	R	S	A	W	P	A	C	T	■	N	I	T	E
O	N	E	■	B	O	L	S	T	E	R	■	D	I	A
K	T	E	L	■	R	E	T	I	R	E	M	E	N	T
S	A	G	E	G	R	E	E	N	■	B	E	R	G	S
■	C	U	T	S	I	N	■	F	A	N	■			
B	L	A	S	T	S	■	O	N	O	■	D	I	S	K
C	A	R	O	■	O	T	H	E	R	W	O	M	A	N
U	R	D	U	■	M	S	M	A	G	A	Z	I	N	E
P	A	S	T	■	E	A	S	T	O	R	A	N	G	E

41

C	L	A	S	P	I	N	G	■	A	N	G	L	E
L	A	S	E	R	B	E	A	M	■	B	O	R	A	X
I	N	A	N	I	M	A	T	E	■	C	R	A	V	E
N	O	R	A	D	■	L	E	T	T	■	Y	O	U	
G	L	U	T	E	I	■	E	A	S	T	E	R	N	
T	I	L	E	■	R	U	M	O	R	H	A	S	I	T
O	N	E	■	C	O	N	A	R	T	I	S	T	S	
■	L	A	N	D	L	I	N	E	S	■				
■	F	O	U	R	L	E	T	T	E	R	■	O	F	T
C	O	I	N	P	U	R	S	E	S	■	B	R	I	E
H	U	L	K	I	N	G	■	S	C	L	E	R	A	
A	L	P	■	G	O	B	S	■	R	A	G	E	S	
I	T	A	L	Y	■	N	O	T	R	E	D	A	M	E
S	I	N	A	I	■	E	Y	E	O	P	E	N	E	R
E	P	S	O	N	■	S	T	E	T	S	O	N	S	

42

A	S	K	O	V	E	R	■	P	T	B	O	A	T	S
R	A	I	S	E	D	A	N	E	Y	E	B	R	O	W
A	L	L	K	I	D	D	I	N	G	A	S	I	D	E
R	O	M	A	N	■	I	N	N	E	R	■	S	I	E
A	M	E	R	■	M	A	J	O	R	■	S	T	E	T
T	E	R	■	T	I	T	A	N	■	K	N	I	F	E
■	B	A	K	E	S	■	D	E	A	D	O	N		
■	I	B	I	S	E	S	■	P	E	E	P	E	R	
A	M	A	Z	E	D	■	M	A	L	L	S	■		
R	I	L	E	D	■	B	U	S	T	S	■	S	H	E
A	T	I	T	■	P	E	S	T	S	■	V	T	E	N
P	A	N	■	S	E	I	K	O	■	K	A	R	A	T
A	T	E	E	N	A	G	E	R	I	N	L	O	V	E
H	O	S	T	I	L	E	T	A	K	E	O	V	E	R
O	R	E	S	T	E	S	■	L	E	E	R	E	R	S

43

```
G E R M I N A T E ■ L U C I A
O V E R T A K E S ■ A N O D E
D O M E S T I C P A R T N E R
I K I D ■ A R S ■ S K I D O O
V E T ■ A L A ■ G A S L O G S
A S S I S I ■ A R P ■ ■ F R O
■ ■ C H A N G E ■ O N E A L
M C G E E ■ O N E ■ P O E M S
A L O E S ■ L E T T E R ■ ■
M E T ■ S A W ■ A R M P I T
M A T D O W N ■ A G A ■ A M Y
A R E O L A ■ E S T ■ A G A R
M I N D I N G T H E S T O R E
I N I G O ■ A R E A C O D E S
A G N E S ■ T E R M I N A T E
```

44

```
S A N T A N A ■ N E T F L I X
C H U N N E L ■ O X I D A T E
A I R T A X I ■ S P R A Y E R
L T S ■ G U M S H O E ■ A M O
D U E T ■ S O L O S ■ T W I X
E N R O N ■ N O W ■ G R A Z E
D A Y L I L Y ■ S P L A Y E D
■ K E Y ■ ■ D I P ■
E T A I L E D ■ I Q T E S T S
N O T E S ■ I N C ■ Z Z T O P
C O E N ■ I V I E S ■ E U R E
A S I ■ A M O E B A S ■ N N E
M O N S T E R ■ A M I S T A D
P O T O M A C ■ T O R P E D O
S N O C O N E ■ H A I R D O S
```

45

```
F A W N ■ A B B A ■ T A S K S
E C H O ■ H E A R ■ I R E N E
M E A T T H E R M O M E T E R
A S T A R ■ T R Y M E ■ T W A
■ H R A P ■ S A G A L ■
P L A Y M E O R T R A D E M E
S A P ■ S O X E R ■ P I S A N
E S P O ■ N Y T O L ■ A T N O
U S E A S ■ G I N O S ■ H O T
D O N T E V E N G O T H E R E
■ S H E E N ■ P I E S ■
C T N ■ K E A T S ■ L Y C E E
W H E R E S T H E R E M O T E
T A X E R ■ E U R O ■ A R A L
S I T E S ■ D R E W ■ N E T S
```

46

```
S T I L L D R E ■ A L B A
C O N E H E A D S ■ M E A N
A R C T A N G E N T ■ O A T S
R E L I S T S ■ O R I E N T E
F A U N A S ■ T W I N B I L L
A D D O N ■ J E T P L A N E
C O E N ■ G A L I L E E
E R S ■ D E S E R E T ■ L O B
■ D E T O X E D ■ J O N I
■ S T E A R N E S ■ T A M E S
T H E O R E M S ■ L I M B I C
Y E S D E A R ■ S A N T A N A
P A S A ■ L A B O R P A R T Y
E T A T ■ Z E N G A R D E N
A H S O ■ L E O N T Y N E
```

47

```
M A D E M I N C E M E A T O F
E C O N O M I C W A R F A R E
L O S A N G E L E S T I M E S
S P E C I A L I N T E R E S T
■ S T E M S ■ I S S ■
■ O D E ■ F F F ■ T R E E
S T U R M ■ B E E F S ■ A X L
M O R S E C O D E S I G N A L
O J S ■ N I L E S ■ L A K M E
G O A L ■ M A X ■ T V S ■
■ U G A ■ P I E R O
C O M M E R C I A L R A D I O
F R E E T R A N S L A T I O N
C H A N S O N S D E G E S T E
S E T S O N A P E D E S T A L
```

48

```
B L U E C R A B ■ L O W F A T
O I L S H A L E ■ B R O O C H
N O N T I T L E ■ J I L T E E
D N A ■ T O R T R E F O R M
■ C L A W C R A N E ■
P A T R O N S A I N T ■ A S A
E B O O K ■ N E C ■ R C A S
T A R N I S H ■ S H T E T L S
A C M E ■ M A O ■ R A I T T
L I E ■ V E L V E T E L V I S
■ F A L L E N H E M ■
E L D O C T O R O W ■ V F W
C O U G A R ■ B R A S S E R A
O R S I N O ■ I M R U I N E D
N I E N T E ■ D E T E N T E S
```

49

```
  D A R E S S A L A A M   █
█ C O N T A C T L E N S E S
W H A T S T H E B I G D E A L
R O S H █ A N T E █ █ F R I A
A L I E N T O █ I N F █ K N T
P E D R O █ O S T E O P A T H
S R O █ N U K E █ A R E T E S
█ █ T O P S E C R E T █ █
S A R D I S █ T O S S █ O Y E
P R E S S E S O N █ E R T E S
E F S █ E T O █ C H E E T O S
N A T E █ B R E A █ T A M A
T R Y T O S E E I T M Y W A Y
█ F L A S H I N T H E P A N █
█ E S T A T E S A L E S █
```

50

```
C A S H B A R S █ K A R S T S
O S C A R W A O █ N I I H A U
N O I F S A N D S O R B U T S
G N A T █ I D I O C Y █ T A S
R E T █ S T R U C K █ M I R E
A M I G A S █ M I I █ O N Y X
T A C O S █ O P E N E D █
S N A P E █ N E T █ D E V A S
█ █ A S M A N Y █ G R A C E
H A P S █ A B T █ P A N G E A
O N I T █ N O O N E R █ A D O
O Y L █ A C U T E R █ A B E T
T H E T R U T H W I L L O U T
C O U R T S █ A L L I A N C E
H O P E S O █ L Y S A N D E R
```

The New York Times

SMART PUZZLES

Presented with Style

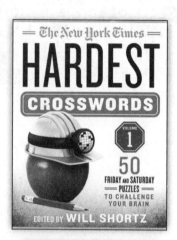

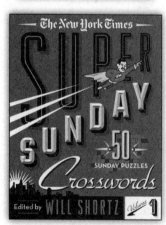